I'M A
WINNER
EITHER WAY

AUSTIN
MULLETT

MileStones
INTERNATIONAL PUBLISHERS

I'm a Winner Either Way

ISBN: 978-1-935870-05-0
UPC: 88571300075-8

Printed in the United States of America.

© 2011 by Austin Mullett, with Duane and Cindy Mullett

MileStones International Publishers
9593 Possum Hollow Road
Shippensburg, PA 17257

303.503.7257; Fax: 717.477.2261

www.milestonesintl.com

1 2 3 4 5 6 7 8 9 10 / 15 14 13 12 11

TABLE OF CONTENTS

A NOTE FROM THE PUBLISHER

Being a publisher for almost three decades, I realize and respect the power of the printed page—especially a book. A book is an amazing thing. It has the power to reach people around the world and the potential for touching the lives of people for many years to come. *I'm a Winner Either Way* is no exception.

Austin Mullett was quite the young man. I first met Austin while in the process of building the concepts for *Big Mountain, Bigger God*, which was written by Austin's parents, Duane and Cindy Mullett. We worked very closely with Austin's family for several months developing these concepts, building foundations and writing this amazing true story of a family who spent their lives traveling the country. They were all very talented musically and devoted their lives to sharing the message of God's love. Throughout Duane and Cindy's entire marriage and ministry, they faced many obstacles. Two of their children, Austin and his younger sister Alisha, shortly after birth, began a very long journey facing major, life-threatening health issues, both having heart transplants as infants, both fighting rejection, Austin fighting life-threatening cancers, Alisha fighting severe allergy issues. Somehow, this family kept it together and continued in ministry proclaiming God's love, faithfulness, and mercy. This was the basis for their first book, *Big Mountain, Bigger God*.

During the long process of personally interviewing each member of the Mullett family, as well as their friends and mentors, I grew to respect Austin. My perception of Austin is that he was a man among men. Although a young teenager, he surprised me with his wit, tenacity, and deep-rooted faith.

Austin most certainly walked the walk of faith and you could sense from every fiber of his being that he truly experienced a relationship with his heavenly Father on a daily basis.

We were in the final stages of writing *Big Mountain, Bigger God* when Austin's health suddenly took a turn for the worse. He ended up spending months in the hospital awaiting his second heart transplant. This first book was very dear to Austin's heart. It tells of the many struggles that he and his family had faced in the past, the present, and what they were about to face in the future. In light of Austin's situation, we made a decision to begin a complete rewrite of the entire story in order to reflect the most current events the Mullett family was facing. At this point, a very large portion of the rewriting process of *Big Mountain, Bigger God* was written in hospital waiting rooms and during extensive medical treatments. It was extremely important to Austin that the message of *Big Mountain, Bigger God* was shared around the world. And he was determined to see the project come to fruition.

I can remember the day that Austin was headed to surgery to receive his second transplant. I cannot imagine how many lives were touched by his strength and courage. While those around him were trying to comfort him and remind him not to be afraid, with a smile on his face, he would say something to the effect of, "I'm not afraid. Just think about it. If I make it through this surgery, I get to spend more time with my family and more time sharing God's love with others. And if I don't make it, I get to be in heaven with my heavenly Father. You see, I'm a winner either way!"

Approximately eight months later, as we were in the final stages of the rewrite for *Big Mountain, Bigger God*, I received word that Austin had unexpectedly died due to complications from his transplant. We immediately restructured the book to include Austin's final days. *Big Mountain, Bigger God* is a very touching true story of one family's faith and proof that God's love, grace, and mercy can carry you through anything you face in life.

Austin's death left my heart broken both for my dear friends the Mulletts, who had lost a son and a brother, and for myself, who had lost a precious young friend.

I was with the family in North Carolina the day they laid Austin to rest. As hundreds of family and friends gathered to reminisce about Austin's life, I was reminded of his strength and determination. Austin had no fear of death and believed that death had no power, that it was just a passageway to a new beginning. I was reminded of Austin's passion to reach the world with the love of God. As we all gathered together to bid our final farewells, I realized for the first time that death was truly a new beginning.

Austin's life moved me. As a publisher, I want to honor his strong beliefs that, when we walk out our daily relationship with God, death truly has no sting and I want to see that his passion to reach the world with God's love can continue.

As we were making our way back home on that cold November day, my mind was flooded with ideas of how to build a new project that would help fulfill Austin's deepest passion. As I was driving through that small town in North Carolina, I was touched by the many different restaurant and church marquees that proclaimed Austin's faith. Some simply said, "Austin Won"; others said, "Austin—A Winner Either Way." I began remembering all the things that Austin and I had discussed and how strongly he believed that death was just a new beginning. Suddenly, in my mind's eye, I saw a large billboard at the edge of their hometown, with giant words proclaiming, "Death Zero, Austin Won!" For me, that was a direct reflection of who Austin was.

Because of his lifetime of illness, some would say that he couldn't take anymore and finally lost the battle. But I know that because of Austin's strong faith, he faced every situation head-on. He fought each fight, ran each race, and won. And that phrase, "Death Zero, Austin Won," helped give birth to this new book that I am certain will touch many lives around the world: *I'm a Winner Either Way*.

This book, *I'm a Winner Either Way*, was made possible by the many family and friends, writers, editors, and graphic agencies who labored together to see to it that Austin's passion and legacy lives on.

—Jim Rill, Publisher

ACKNOWLEDGMENTS

I was only 16 years old when I made my transition from earth to heaven. From the beginning, my life was filled with two heart transplants, the fight to win the battle of terminal cancers, and ongoing procedures to battle organ rejection, infection, and coinciding health issues. There were also times between procedures that my strength was returned and I could live somewhat of a normal life.

My mom and dad have always had a passion to reach the world with the love of God. At a very young age, I realized in my heart that for me there was nothing more satisfying than sharing God's love with others. My family and I would travel the country in ministry and music and, in my lifetime, I have seen many lives changed as people accepted the message of God's love.

There are so many hurting and lonely people in this world. There are those facing medical situations, those who have lost loved ones, and those who are facing mountains in their life that seem far too big to ever cross over. There are many desperate people who in their heart wonder, "Will the sun ever shine again in my life?" At a young age, I realized that no matter what you face in life, having a true relationship with your heavenly Father will always carry you through. It had become my lifetime passion to share this love with as many people around the world that I could. Although my life on earth has been cut short, I always held strong to the fact that death has no sting, death has no power, life on earth is but a vapor, and death is really a new beginning.

Like I said, I am only 16 years old. Please understand that some of the concepts that I have embraced in this book are concepts that I have not fully achieved. I was in the learning process and I was working to build a foundation with the concepts discussed in each chapter.

I would like to thank my family, friends, and mentors, as well as the publishing professionals who have helped shape my thoughts and words into this book. Without you this project would never have come to fruition. Thank you for believing in me and for your hard work in giving me a voice from my new home in heaven. My family has said many times, "Death is not the end; death is a new beginning." Because of your support, my dreams and passions to reach the world with the message of God's unfailing love has been made possible.

Some of the people who were the most influential in my life were, of course, my mom and dad. My sisters, Brianna, Alisha, Chantaya, and Kyra, were my best friends and I am so grateful to God for the relationship I had with them. I appreciate the godly examples of my grandparents, Henry and Ada Coblentz and John and Merlyn Mullett. Some of the men whom I admired the most who were in my lifetime and whose teachings and examples I was honored to apply in my own life were:

Bill Gothard	Ken Ham
Billy Graham	Nelson Coblentz
Chip Ingram	Dr. Joel Robbins
Ray Comfort	Otto Koning

FOREWORD
"A GIFT FROM GOD"

Although Austin was granted only a little less than 17 years of life on this earth, he crammed into those years more life experiences than do many people four times older than he. Because health was an issue all his life, Austin developed an attitude and understanding of life and death, of mortality and immortality, that was much more mature and advanced than that of most people his age. As a result, Austin knew how to appreciate life and enjoy it to the fullest, even the simplest pleasures. He had a zest for life and loved to celebrate anything! In our family, Austin was always the life of the party. He loved to tell funny stories and play practical jokes on each of us. It is so easy, especially as adults, to get so caught up with the burdens and concerns of everyday living and circumstances that we lose sight of the big picture: that life is good. Austin was always there to remind us of this, and by his own example bring us back to a positive perspective. He loved life despite the boundaries that his ongoing health issues imposed. For example, although he loved sports, Austin often was unable to play because of his health. Rather than sulk or complain or become depressed, he found other ways to stay involved, such as coaching or keeping score.

Austin's positive outlook on life was never clearer than in the way he faced his tremendous health challenges. Those challenges began early in his life. Before Austin was a year old, he underwent a heart transplant because of a genetic condition that damaged and severely weakened his original heart. Less than a month after his 16th birthday, he underwent a second one. The years in between were filled with countless medical tests, evaluations, and procedures. His body was poked and prodded too many times to count. Austin became very familiar with needles, IV catheters, pic lines, spinal taps, and just about any other invasive and painful medical procedure you could imagine. We still have Austin's "Beads of Courage," two strings of beads, each one several feet long, that represent his medical history. One string represents his experiences through everything related to his two life-threatening heart transplants, and the other string represents his two bouts with aggressive cancer as a young boy that he faced and conquered. Each bead on the strings represents a different hospital procedure Austin endured (IVs, blood work, surgeries, ICU visits, spinal taps, biopsies, etc.). Some of the beads stand for 10 or even 50 times of going through a particular procedure.

Because he was a transplant patient, Austin was on a continual regimen of anti-rejection medication, which required that his immune system be suppressed. This state of affairs made him unusually vulnerable to all sorts of sicknesses, including cancer. By the grace of God and highly focused medical (and nutritional) treatment, including aggressive chemotherapy, Austin conquered the cancers that invaded his body. He knew how it felt to get the devastating news that his cancer was back and it was going to be a long road to recovery. He also knew what it was like for a 15-year-old to be told that he was in congestive heart failure and that, at any given time, he could go into heart arrest and die.

Yet through it all, Austin demonstrated a courageous spirit that inspired all of us. No matter how inconvenient or painful a procedure was, Austin was never a complainer, particularly as he grew older and was able to understand more fully what was happening to him. He learned to look for the positive in every situation. Even when he was being wheeled to the operating room for a second heart transplant, he had a smile on his face! He was ready to get it done and move on. Besides, he knew that the very worst that could happen was that he would die in surgery or shortly thereafter, and then he would be with Jesus. So why worry?

Austin had a peaceful spirit that grew from his deep love and absolute confidence in his heavenly Father, which, in turn, grew out of the close relationship he had with Duane, his earthly father. From the very beginning, Duane and Austin enjoyed an especially deep and secure father/son relationship (which you will read more about in the pages that follow), which made it easy for Austin, while still a young boy, to receive the love of his heavenly Father by accepting Jesus Christ as his personal Savior and Lord. It was this multidimensional father/son relationship—the earthly and heavenly—that was the source of Austin's uncommon peace of mind and optimism, even during the most difficult, painful, or uncertain circumstances. Austin knew he was loved, he knew that he was safe and secure, and no matter what happened, he knew where he was going.

Whatever Austin may have lacked in physical strength, he more than made up for in mental strength. Austin was blessed with great intelligence. He was a voracious reader and a quick learner who excelled as a home-schooler. For each of his last three to four years of schooling, his yearly achievement tests scored him as being at a 13th grade equivalent or higher. He was also a computer whiz and loved to use his computer and technical abilities to help others. There were times even in the hospital when he would assist another young patient with solving computer problems. For Austin, time was too precious to waste reading about superficial things, so he focused on the Bible, books that had spiritual depth, and "self-help" books. He also enjoyed reading (and mastering) computer books. He especially enjoyed reading about heroes of the Christian faith, people such as John Wesley, David Livingstone, Billy Sunday, C.S. Lewis, Brother Andrew, Jim Elliot, and others.

Regarding family, Austin took his position and example as the firstborn child very seriously. He had four younger sisters whom he loved deeply, and the feeling was mutual. He was always thinking of tangible ways to show his love for his sisters and was always sensitive to the sacrifices that often were required of them because of his ongoing health issues. A special bond existed between Austin and his second sister, Alisha, who, like Austin, had a heart transplant when she was only a few months old.

Because of their similar health issues, there were times when Austin and Alisha had to go in for certain tests or procedures at the same time. Austin always volunteered to go first to encourage Alisha that anything they faced was tolerable and that everything would be fine. This was true even when it came to death. Austin went first, and today Alisha no longer fears death as she once did. Her big brother has gone before, and she knows that if he could speak to her audibly from the other side he would say, "Don't worry, everything is fine."

In October 2010, after a brief illness, Austin went home to the heavenly Father whom he had loved for so long, leaving behind a shocked and grieving family. Together we stood beside the open grave on that cold November afternoon, numb to everything but the agonizing grief that seared our hearts, watching with tear-filled eyes as the casket was lowered, consigning the physical body—the empty shell—of our son and brother to the earth. We knew in our hearts that Austin was with Jesus, and that he was free and whole and happy, yet the pain of his passing would not release us. Grief clung to us like an oppressive late winter snow.

Only a week earlier Austin had been vibrantly alive, laughing and joking. Now all was quiet. As we stood there beside the mound of dirt covered with flowers, a gentle breeze passed by. And we heard it—as from a far distance, as light as the barest scent of lilies on the breeze—Austin's voice, singing, "I'm a Winner Either Way."

Today, though we feel that Austin's time with us was much too short, we also know that God's timing is never wrong. And although we miss him deeply, we take comfort in the fact that today he is happier, healthier, and more alive than ever before, and we of his family who remain behind look forward to the day when we will be reunited with him in God's new creation.

We have said all we need to say. Now it is time to let Austin speak for himself. There are many things he wants to say to you and, as you will discover, he has a unique and insightful perspective on things. It is our hope and prayer that you will be blessed by the conversation. We believe you will be.

—Duane and Cindy Mullett

INTRODUCTION

"Austin…You are a gift from God…A young man in whom I am well pleased. You are my firstborn and one of eternal significance. You are the one who is 'worthy of honor' as you daily lay down your personal wishes and follow the voice of God. You are a young man of faith in an Almighty God. That faith is demonstrated by your confidence in God after facing difficulties. Faith helps you to rise after a fall and in so doing, you bring glory to God. Many will be brought to faith in God by your obedience and faithfulness. Christ in you gives you hope. I love you…Your Dad"

This is the blessing that my Dad spoke regularly into my life. Mom and Dad realized years ago the importance of speaking a blessing into their children. Proverbs 18:21 says, "The tongue has the power of life and death, and those who love it will eat its fruit." They firmly believed— and taught the five of us children to believe—that in so many ways we all are the result of what someone else has spoken into us, whether good or bad. Mom and Dad wanted to make sure that I and my four sisters each knew how very unique, special, and precious we were, and how God had a specific plan for each of us that no one else could fulfill. With this in mind, they wrote up a blessing for each of us that took into account the meaning of our name and our God-given personality to express to us their prayer for our life and their vision of how they felt God would be able to use each of us most effectively. I will never forget the impact this blessing had on me when I was growing up. It always made me feel warm and happy inside because I knew I was loved not only by my parents, but even more by God. It was during many of my darkest and lowest times—when I was sick, or in severe pain from surgery or some medical procedure, or weak from chemotherapy, or when I was feeling useless because I was too sick and weak to help out with chores at home—that the words of my Dad's blessing would come to mind, lift my spirits, and restore my perspective. Words like: "You are a gift from God...one of eternal significance...one who is worthy of honor...a young man of faith." My dad's blessing was instrumental in shaping me into the person I became, a foretaste of the wholeness in Christ that I now enjoy in full. In fact, Dad usually puts his hand on my sisters' shoulders or puts his arm around them when he gives them his blessing, but I wasn't satisfied with just that. I wanted to sit on his lap and totally be in his embrace when he gave me his blessing. What a small picture this is of the joy I am now experiencing in my heavenly Father's embrace!

Instead of always pointing out to us children the things we were doing wrong, Mom and Dad attempted to speak blessings into our lives that focused on the character qualities that God wanted to develop in us. We spent each month studying a specific character quality and looked for ways to apply them into each of our lives. This was a dynamic tool that influenced me to develop into a young man of faith. Never underestimate the power of words; they can make or break your destiny, or the destiny of the ones you love.

CHAPTER 1

DESPERATE FOR "DADDY"

When was the last time life hit you with something you couldn't handle? You say that's never happened to you? Come on now, don't deny it; I know better! We all like to believe that we've got everything under control no matter what life throws at us. That's only human. The last thing we want is for somebody else to think that we don't have it all together. To have to admit, "I need help; I can't do this by myself," goes against every instinct in our mind. Our pride insists, "I can take whatever you've got. Hit me with your best shot." But sometimes we can't. Sometimes life throws a curve ball we just can't hit or a punch we just can't dodge. Sooner or later, if it hasn't happened already, life will sneak up on you and slam you with something that is more than you can take. It'll make you feel like you've been knocked out of a boat without a life preserver only to discover that you don't know how to swim. Then what will you do? Will you keep on insisting, "I'm okay; I can do this; everything's fine," even as you're sinking beneath the waves? Or will you pull in your pride long enough to shout, "Help!"?

Although things are completely different for me now, during my almost 17 years of life on earth there was never a day that went by when I was not dependent upon someone else for something. I have no memories of my first heart transplant; I was way too little when it happened! From the very beginning I grew up knowing that there were certain things I simply could not do without assistance...and some things that I could not do at all because of my bodily limitations. Since I had never known anything else, this seemed natural to me. It wasn't until my sister Brianna came along, who had no health problems, or when I saw other kids enjoying things I was not strong enough to do, that I really became aware of how different my situation was. I don't think I ever resented it. After my second heart transplant, I needed help to get out of bed and couldn't even attend to my personal needs by myself. My dad would help me with that. My mom would wash and comb my hair while I sat on a chair since I was unable to shower yet at this point. This could have been very difficult for other 16-year-olds to accept, but I thanked my parents for helping me and never complained about my situation. After all, that's just how things were, and I accepted it. There would be no content for this book if it wasn't for the difficulties that I encountered! You would not be inspired by the magnitude of God's grace that was so evident in my life if not for the magnitude of my sufferings.

The people I looked to the most to help me through the things I couldn't do alone were, naturally, Mom and Dad. This was especially true during the many times that I was sick or in the hospital or required a certain test or procedure. As far back as I can remember, Mom and Dad were always there to hold me, comfort me, encourage me, and help me understand what was going on. I loved my mom (and still do!), but Dad and I had a very special relationship. It seems that at the times when I was at my sickest, I wanted Dad there with me. Dad was with me when I went through all my chemotherapy treatments for the two cancers I had when I was six or seven years old. (Mom had to take care of my sisters.) I came to the place where I wanted Dad with me whenever I had to have any tough procedure done. Whenever I was very sick or experiencing something very painful, I always wanted to make sure that Dad was right there beside me. I guess you could say I was desperate for Dad. I didn't want to let Dad out of my sight because I knew that as long as Dad was there, I would be all right. He would hold my hand, pray with me, and hold me down during a painful procedure and talk gently to me, calming me down and helping me understand what they were doing and why it was necessary. It didn't make the pain any less, but it was more bearable because Dad was there. I trusted him and he never let me down. When I was younger, Mom was always with me for my hospital visits and on more than one occasion they would have to work for a long time to get an IV into my tiny veins. They would even have to try to get one in my forehead! I was crying so much and looking up at Mom with a pleading look on my face for her to protect me. It broke Mom's heart! Although she so badly wanted to be there for me, she just couldn't bear seeing me suffer and not be able to do something about it. At those times, Dad would tell her, "You can leave the room. I will stay here with him. He will be fine." Mom was there to comfort me after they were done. Through both of my parents, I saw a small glimpse of who God was. My dad was always constant and I never had to face a situation alone and my mom was caring and compassionate and ready to encourage me on. Because of Dad, I made it through hundreds of tough and unpleasant situations that I could never have handled alone. Because of Dad, I learned

> *I learned that when you have a close relationship with your heavenly Father, you can bear up under anything...and if your trouble is more than you can bear, He will carry you.*

that when you have a close relationship with your heavenly Father, you can bear up under anything...and if your trouble is more than you can bear, He will carry you.

I remember one time when I was about seven years old coming home from the hospital with Dad after one of my extensive chemotherapy sessions. Chemotherapy was supposed to involve several days of intensive treatment in the hospital followed by several weeks of recuperation at home until it was time for the next treatment. However, the protocol didn't work that way for me. I was usually only home for one night and then the next day I would have a fever because of low white cell counts. This meant I needed to be hospitalized again and so back we went to the sterile floor where I was surrounded by other children with no hair and and facing painful procedures again. My parents tried to shield me from the awareness of some of these children not surviving, but they were not always able to do it. I saw firsthand the ravaging effects of this monster we call cancer! Although the medications worked and helped drive my cancer into remission, they also had the side effect of leaving me very weak, exhausted, and physically drained. Many times it took my entire recuperation time in the hospital just to build up enough strength for the next treatment session. One particular time, Dad and I got home and started walking up the steps from the downstairs garage to the house. Dad had his arms full with all of our hospital belongings. I wanted so much to help out by carrying something, but I was too weak. My legs hurt a lot from some of the medication I had been given during my chemotherapy. They were so weak and painful that I could barely get myself up the steps.

In fact, I couldn't do it. My legs started shaking and I felt what little strength I had left draining away. Suddenly that next step looked like it was about a mile high. I knew I couldn't walk any farther, so I got down on my hands and knees and started to crawl. I only made it up a few more steps before I realized that wasn't going to work either. By this time Dad was almost at the top of the stairs. I called out to him, "I can't make it anymore, Daddy. Can you carry me?" Immediately, Dad set down the things he had been carrying and hurried down the steps to me. He had tears in his eyes as he scooped me up in his arms, held me close to his chest, and took me inside. I could have kept on struggling to make it up the steps on my own, but when my strength was gone, and when life at that moment was too much for me, I knew Dad was there to pick me up and carry me.

That's the kind of relationship your heavenly Father wants you to have with Him. Are you, like I was, stuck in the middle of the stairway of a situation that is too big for you, and you can't take another step? Do you know your heavenly Father well enough to know that He will never ask more of you then you can handle with His help? The Bible says, *"I can do everything through him who gives me strength"* (Phil. 4:13). Did you hear that? Everything! God gives you the strength to do everything you need to do in life, and in His strength you can overcome any obstacle. So why are you crawling on the hands and knees of your own strength, getting weaker by the minute? Call out to "Daddy"! He will carry you through.

> *Why are you crawling on the hands and knees of your own strength, getting weaker by the minute? Call out to "Daddy"! He will carry you through.*

So whatever punch life is throwing your way, don't just "man up," grit your teeth, and get ready to take it on the chin. Don't try to tough it out on your own saying, "I can handle this." What if you can't? Why take the chance? If there's one thing that my earthly father and grandfathers taught me, it is that real men love God. Real men need Jesus. Real men know where their limitations are and aren't afraid to say so.

Whatever problem you're facing, don't face it alone. Call out to your heavenly Father and let Him help you. And even if life is going smoothly for you right now, use this time to get to know your heavenly Father. Pray to Him. Spend time with Him. Take time to let Him speak to you. It is because I saw my dad and got to know him during the good times that I knew I could trust him to be there for me in the hard times. Had it not been for that relationship, I might have thought that I had no choice but to struggle on my own. It's the same way with God. In fact, I believe it is like my dad always says, "Your personal relationship with your heavenly Father is truly validated by your response to Him during the times of difficulties." If you spend time getting to know your heavenly Father during the good times in your life, you will find that you will automatically turn to Him when you are facing the difficult and painful things in life...and you will find Him right there ready to strengthen, help, and uphold you with His hand, so that you can do everything in His strength. And unlike even the best earthly father, God has no boundaries to His love or restrictions to how He can help you. When you put your heart in His hands, you can trust Him through all of life's circumstances—the good, the bad, and the ugly. You just can't lose. In

His hands you are a winner either way! Believe me, from where I am sitting right now, I know this is true. Just wait 'til you get here! You haven't seen anything yet!

Get desperate for your Daddy!

SPECIAL NOTE TO DADS

I know I am only 16 years old. A lot of people would say that that is still a very young age and what could I really know about adult matters such as manhood and being a father and provider for a family? What could I possibly know about all of the things that a man must face in today's world—the stress, the worry, and the fear of tomorrow, coupled with being wild at heart? You want to win, you want to prosper, and you want to be seen as a strong force in whatever you do. Unfortunately, in today's day and age, it becomes far too easy to overlook what is really important in life. There are milestones that a man has always looked forward to. It starts at a very early age. You have heard the sayings, "I can't wait 'til I'm big enough to do that. I can't wait 'til I'm sixteen and I can drive. I can't wait 'til I'm twenty-one...." Many can't wait to get married, buy a home, have a good job, and have their first child. I am sure that when that time comes there is no other dream bigger than being the best daddy that you can be. And you can't wait to partake in the childlike wonder of being young again as you watch your newborn baby grow from day to day. But in light of many circumstances that we face in life, after a short period of time it is far too easy to treat your child, and in some cases even your wife, kind of like you would treat a used car. The newness and the excitement is very easily halted by the demands of this world. Your job, social status, and sometimes selfishness become more prevalent in your heart than the excitement that you first had holding your newborn child. You hear the warnings and deep down you feel the urge to get back to the basic fundamentals of being a good father and a good husband. But it is clouded by your desire to perform; therefore, it is easy to become insensitive to the true needs of that child. Whether you like it or not, your child is desperate for Daddy. Every day, the power of your actions and the power of your words are etched on that child's heart for life. The child seems to be extremely resilient and forgiving and always seems to bounce back in love. But let me warn you. Time on this earth and time with your family, and especially your children, moves very swiftly, literally like sand through your fingers. I challenge you: find a beach or a sandbox, scoop your hands through it, and watch the sand sift through your hands. Watch it very carefully because that is life. Too often it is easy for a Daddy to say, "I'll do better tomorrow." And when tomorrow gets here, it's the next day, then the next day, and then the next....

I want to let you know, from a young person's perspective, how desperate children are for your love and your affection. To them, you are their hero. When you get angry with them and you hurt them with words, a few minutes later you are still their hero. If they ask you to play, but you don't have time, a few minutes later you are still their hero. If they just want to spend time with you and you just don't have the time, you are still their hero. I know children who have been extremely, physically abused, yet somehow their heart still sees the abuser as a hero. Why? Because they are desperate for Daddy.

As you read these words, I challenge you to go to the mirror, look deep into your eyes, and try to remember what's really important in life. Try to remember the sand sifting through your fingers. Try to remember the joy of the first time you held your child in your arms. Try to remember that tomorrow may never come and today is all that matters. Ask God to help you live for today and reestablish true love in your heart, to help you to see the important role that you play in a young child's life. Think about it. What's so hard about taking your son for a ride to the park? What's so hard about having a special dinner date with your little girl? What's so hard about understanding a child's excitement when he catches his first bug? And why is it that you are simply too tired to toss a couple of balls when your child wants to play? Your teenager also needs you. He needs to know that he is significant to you and that you understand the struggles he is facing because you have struggles as well. If you look at the root issues, many times you see your children struggle in the same areas you are struggling. Are you taking the time to hear your child's heart cry? You may say, "My family has a home to live in. We have money to spend and we have food to eat. My child has every toy imaginable." And that is honorable. But I want you to remember the following words because they are the words that mean the most in life: "Daddy, look at me.

Daddy, listen to me." How important it is to really look and really listen to the heart of your child. The sad truth is, there are many fathers around the world who have been crippled by grief, and if they had just one more chance, they would take the ride, the special date, toss a few balls, and if given the opportunity, just one more chance to hold that child close. Tomorrow is here and their child is gone. Live for today and remember, your child is desperate for Daddy. Get desperate for them!

CHAPTER 2

EMBRACE YOUR BOUNDARIES

One of the most basic lessons we all have to learn in life is how to live within boundaries. This does not come naturally for most of us. We would all like to believe that we have no boundaries; that we can do anything we want anytime we want without limitations. However, complete freedom of action does not exist for anyone, and those who try to push the limits too far suffer the consequences. My family visited many prisons during our concert and ministry tours, and every one of them was filled with people who were paying the price for their choice to violate the established boundaries of law and society.

If you think about it, life is all about boundaries. Someone has said that 90% of life consists of things we can neither control nor change. If this is true, it means that we can control, alter, or change our circumstances or conditions only 10% of the time. One reason so many people are unhappy and dissatisfied in life is that they spend all their time butting their heads against the 90% that they cannot change while ignoring the 10% that they can change. There is just something about us humans that resist the idea of limitations. In one sense this is a good thing because it can lead to "possibility" thinking or "out-of-the-box" thinking, which in turn can lead to innovations that blow away what was once thought to be a genuine limitation. Resisting boundaries is a bad thing, however, when it causes us to ignore reality. Like it or not, there are some things we simply cannot change, some boundaries we simply cannot cross. One of our biggest challenges is learning to tell the difference. And once we do, the next

The big challenge is learning to make the most of life within the boundaries we cannot change.

big challenge is learning to make the most of life within the boundaries we cannot change.

All my life on earth I lived with more physical boundaries than most young people. I'm sure many people wondered how I dealt with it. Some even asked me, "How do you cope with it? How do you handle the reality of knowing that you can't do a lot of the things other kids your age do?" To be perfectly honest, that was not as big an issue with me as many might expect, mainly because I never knew anything else. Having received my first heart transplant as a very young baby, I had no memories of a day without specific physical limitations. I learned to live with them because that was the reality of my life.

This doesn't mean that it never bothered me; sometimes it did. As I grew older and became interested in various sports, such as basketball or baseball, I played whenever I had the chance, but I often had to stop earlier than the others because I lacked the physical stamina to play as long or as hard as they did. Sometimes, particularly after being in the hospital, after certain medical procedures or while I was in congestive heart failure, I was too weak to play at all. The only thing I could do was watch all the others having fun and wish I could be out there with them. It was during times like these that I was most likely to feel discouraged and disappointed. My parents were a great help to me in learning how to deal with those feelings and with the reality of my limitations.

Basically, I had two choices. One, I could dwell on my limitations, butting my head against the 90% that I could not change; get frustrated, discouraged, angry, and bitter; and make my life miserable. Or, on the other hand, I could focus on finding ways to make the most of life within my limitations. For example, many times when I was physically unable to play basketball or baseball, I still participated by keeping score. That was something I could do, and it was a lot more fun and productive than going off by myself somewhere to mope. It didn't take me long to learn that the second choice was always better. I probably enjoyed life the most of any of my family! My motto was, Why focus on all of the things that are going wrong when you can focus on so many things that are going great! I was often aware that the doctors said I had a shorter life expectancy. Since I didn't want it weighing over me like some curse, my goal was to be the longest living heart transplant patient. I know I didn't achieve it, but this perspective sure was better than feeling like I had a death sentence hanging over me. I savored the journey that I was on!

One of my favorite poems that was a comfort to me was entitled, "Mr. Tentmaker." I hope that it will bless you as well.

Mr. Tentmaker

It was nice living in this tent when it was strong and secure

and the sun was shining and the air was warm.

But Mr. Tentmaker it's scary now.

You see my tent is acting like it is not going to hold together;

the poles seem weak and they shift with the wind.

A couple of the stakes have wiggled loose from the sand;

and worst of all, the canvas has a rip.

It no longer protects me from beating rain or stinging flies.

It's scary in here Mr. Tentmaker.

Last week I went to the repair shop and some repairman

tried to patch the rip in my canvas.

It didn't help much, though, because the patch pulled away from

the edges and now the tear is worse.

What troubles me most, Mr. Tentmaker, is that the repairman didn't

even seem to notice that I was still in the tent;

he just worked on the canvas while I shivered inside.

I cried out once, but no one heard me.

I guess my first real question is: Why did you give me such a flimsy tent?

I can see by looking around the campground that some of the tents are

much stronger and more stable than mine.

Why, Mr. Tentmaker, did you pick a tent of such poor quality for me?

And even more important, what do you intend to do about it?

Oh little tent dweller, as the Creator and Provider of tents,

I know all about you and your tent, and I love you both.

I made a tent for Myself once, and lived in it on your campground.

My tent was vulnerable, too, and some vicious attackers ripped it to pieces

while I was still in it.

It was a terrible experience, but you will be glad to know they couldn't hurt me;

in fact, the whole occurrence was a tremendous advantage

because it is this very victory over my enemy that frees me

to be a present help to you.

*O little tent dweller, I am now prepared to come and live
    in your tent with you,*

if you'll invite me.

You'll learn as we dwell together that real security comes from

my being in your tent with you.

*When the storms come, you can huddle in my arms and I'll
    hold you.*

When the canvas rips, we'll go to the repair shop together.

*Someday, little tent dweller, someday your tent is going to
    collapse;*

you see, I've designed it only for temporary use.

But when it does, you and I are going to leave together,

I promise not to leave before you do.

And then free of all that would hinder or restrict,

we will move to our permanent home and together, forever,

we will rejoice and be glad.

—Anonymous

Another way I tried to make the most of life within my limitations was to stop worrying about the things I could not do very well (even if other kids my age could) and devote my time and energy to the things I could do well. My physical body often did not cooperate with me, but that did not affect my mind. My physical body may have been weak, but God blessed me with a good mind, and I always tried to find ways to improve the mental talents that God had given me. I loved to read and spend time on the computer. I spent hours and hours using the library and the Internet to learn as much as I could about many different things. I also discovered that I was good with technical things, such as fixing computer problems, so I always looked for ways to help people with those problems. These were things I could do even while confined to a hospital bed, and I spent many of my waking hours doing just that. I loved it when people would bring me a computer they couldn't unlock or had viruses on them and I was able, within a few minutes, to have it all taken care of. Even at home, I was not able to help Mom and Dad with much of the physical work, but they always came to me if they had a computer question or problem. There were many things I could not do, but I could do computers, so I always gave it my best.

One of the keys to happiness and contentment in life is learning not just to accept the genuine boundaries in your life but even to embrace those boundaries. The more you accept your personal limitations and weaknesses, the more God can use you to touch the lives of people in a unique way. I always found inspiration and encouragement in the life and example of Joni Eareckson Tada. Talk about limitations! Crippled in a diving accident, Joni Eareckson Tada has been a quadriplegic since she was a teenager, yet she embraced those physical boundaries, becoming a highly acclaimed artist by learning to paint and draw with her mouth. At the same time, she has devoted her life to telling others, by both word and example, of the grace and love of God and how He can use anyone who surrenders his or her life to Him.

> *One of the keys to happiness and contentment in life is learning not just to accept the genuine boundaries in your life but even to embrace those boundaries.*

God is not limited by your limitations; on the contrary, if you let Him, He will take you beyond your limitations. What I mean by this is that if you embrace your boundaries, whatever they are—if you adopt a positive attitude toward your limitations and see them as opportunities rather than liabilities—God can use you to impact the lives of people to a far greater degree than you could ever do by yourself in your own weakness. Embracing your boundaries will help you learn to trust in God's resources and power rather than your own. I think that's what the apostle Paul meant when he wrote:

> *To keep me from becoming conceited because of these surpassingly great revelations, there was given me a thorn in my flesh, a messenger of Satan, to torment me. Three times I pleaded with the Lord to take it away from me. But he said to me, "My grace is sufficient for you, for my power is made perfect in weakness." Therefore I will boast all the more gladly about my weaknesses, so that Christ's power may rest on me. That is why, for Christ's sake, I delight in weaknesses, in insults, in hardships, in persecutions, in difficulties. For when I am weak, then I am strong* (2 Corinthians 12:7-10).

God's power is made perfect in our weakness. That means that when we embrace our boundaries and allow God to work through us in spite of our limitations, people will see His power and His glory more clearly because our strength and our pride and our efforts will not be standing in the way. When we surrender our lives to the Lord, His strength makes us strong. Someone once said that "We are stronger weak than when we are strong." One of my favorite Bible verses that always encouraged me is Philippians 4:13: *"I can do all things through Christ who strengthens me"* (NKJV™).

Don't let your boundaries define who you are or what you can or cannot do. Instead, let God define you; after all, He created you and knows everything there is to know about you. Regardless of the genuine limitations or boundaries there may be in your life, God has still gifted and equipped you with talents and abilities that, in His power, can take you farther than you ever imagined. Your possibilities are virtually unlimited because He is the God of the impossible! And remember, every miracle that ever took place first started with an impossibility!

In life, I ran my race. I ran as hard as I could. And I won the race! I embraced my boundaries and trusted

God to take me to new limits that on my own I could never accomplish. No matter what you face in life, your strength comes when you run to Him. That's all that I could do. So I ran and I ran, one step in front of the other, right into His arms. I found that whether in life or in death, in His arms you cannot lose. I'm a winner either way!

CHAPTER 3

GOD IS STILL GOOD

In my family's extensive concert and preaching tours through the years, we visited many churches and prisons, sharing the good news of Jesus Christ through music and the spoken word. One statement that I heard over and over from many different people in many different places really resonated with me because it reflected what I already believed: "God is good all the time, and all the time, God is good." That just about says it all. And it really is true. God is good, and He is good all the time.

Okay, I know. I hear somebody out there saying, "But, Austin, how can you say that God is good? After all you went through, after two heart transplants, and two bouts with cancer, and all those painful tests and procedures throughout the years, God still let you die when you were only 16 years old, with practically your whole life before you."

Well, that's one way to look at it, I guess. But that is such a limited viewpoint. Here's how I see it: God did not "let" me die when I was "only" 16 and had my whole life ahead of me; rather, He granted me early access to a life that is fuller and greater than anything any of us could ever truly imagine on earth; a life of unlimited possibilities that has no end. Isn't it amazing how different things look when you see them from God's point of view? It's all a matter of perspective. If we believe that heaven is our reward, then didn't God just allow me to receive my reward earlier? Now I know that my family misses me terribly and I have the greater advantage but I also know that they have been able to see so many ways that God has used my "home-going" to benefit their lives as well. It doesn't seem logical to our human minds, I know, but there are benefits and good that can come out of every difficult circumstance. A few of those benefits for my family have been the following: a greater awareness and yearning for heaven, a greater appreciation for each day they have with each other, and a stronger desire and capability to comfort others who are sorrowing. I challenge you to list the benefits that you see in each of the trials you are facing. We often quote Romans 8:28: *"And we know that all things work together for good to those who love God…"* (NKJV™). Yet we don't go on to the next verse where it says that He works it for our good, *"…to be **conformed** to the image of His Son"* (NKJV™, emphasis added). What is your definition of things working for your good? So often our view of God's goodness is defined by what makes us happy and comfortable. If we have this "man-centered" view of God, then what will we think of God when tragedies come our way? We will question His goodness! Because we live in a fallen world, we face the results and experience sin, death, and sorrows. This was not God's plan, since He never intended for His beautiful creation to suffer. It grieves His "Daddy" heart when anyone endures any level of pain. It was because of His love that He created us with a choice to love or reject Him. This choice opened the door for all the many tragic and devastating consequences that are the result of rejecting Him and His perfect plan for us. God has to allow the consequences of sin or He would not be a just God.

How you look at the world and at your circumstances depends on your vantage point. If all you see are your problems and troubles looming over you like a tall mountain that is blocking your way, then it is not surprising if you feel discouraged and hopeless and ready to give up. That's when you need to change your perspective and learn to see your situation the way God does. From the ground, that mountain looks impossible to climb, just like those stairs from the garage to the house that day after chemotherapy when I was too weak to go any farther by myself. But when you let God pick you up and you get a God's-eye view of the situation, you realize that from up there that mountain does not look so tall after all. Not only that, but you can also see that just on the other side of the mountain is a gorgeous green valley. And running between your side of the mountain and the valley on the other side is a passageway that you cannot see when you are right in the middle of your situation at ground level. But God sees it. Perspective is everything. It's easy to become afraid and depressed. Many give up too soon, so overwhelmed that they feel as if the sun will never shine again. They can't see beyond the mountain. We all face desperate situations where we are blinded to hope—until we allow God to lift us up to the high place that reveals a more realistic perspective of what now seems to be an impossible situation.

Trust God with your circumstances, and He will see you through every time. You will never know the truth of a situation until you see it from God's point of view.

I learned early on that there were many things in life I could not control and that it was useless to try. So I learned to focus on the things I could change. For example, although I could not change the reality that I had to go into the hospital for a biopsy or some other painful procedure, I could control my attitude and response to that reality. I could whine and fuss and cry and complain and get all "woe is me" about that particular mountain, or I could take a higher view

You will never know the truth of a situation until you see it from God's point of view.

and look ahead in anticipation to the green valley beyond: being able to go back home and celebrate the fact that it was over and that the doctors had learned something that would help them treat me so that I could get better.

What I am saying is that many times we cannot control what happens to us in life, but we can control how we respond to what happens to us. The reality may be beyond our control, but our response is not; we choose how to respond. When we have godly character, we look beyond our circumstances and sorrows. We sail right through the storm clouds into the bright sunshine, which always awaits us on the other side. We seem to forget that that the sweetest joys of life are the fruits of sorrow. Just as a torch burns brighter when waved back and forth and as juniper smells the sweetest when it is being consumed by flames, so the richest qualities of God's children arise under the strong winds of suffering and adversity.

About now some of you are probably thinking, "But, Austin, what does all of this have to do with the goodness of God?" Everything. Whatever situation you are in, good or bad, you can choose to trust God in it or not to trust God. You can choose to see God working in and through your situation for your good and His glory, or you can choose not to see Him working. The choice is yours. Due in large part to Mom and Dad's example, I learned early in life to believe and trust completely in the goodness of God. I saw His goodness every day in the love and care they showed to me and to my sisters. I saw His goodness in the way they were always right by my side during the hardest, most painful, and scariest times of my life. I saw His goodness in the way He cared for them through all the visits, phone calls, e-mails, web postings, and other gestures of support they received, especially in the times when they were the most discouraged and tired. I saw His goodness in the multitude of answered prayers, and in the times He carried me safely through dangerous surgeries and other procedures, and through many emergency health crises where I easily could have died. I saw His goodness in the loving and warm fellowship that my parents, my sisters, and I enjoyed as a family. Most of all, I saw His goodness in the knowledge that He sent His Son, Jesus Christ, to die on the cross for my sins, so that I could be forgiven and become His son through a new birth into His likeness.

And from where I sit today, I know that my faith in God's goodness was not mistaken. When I was on earth, I believed God was good, but I did not know the half of it! You'll have to trust me on this, but the full truth of the goodness of God is beyond comprehension from the limited perspective of earthly life! I now know truly what the apostle Paul meant when he wrote: *"No eye has seen, no ear has heard, no mind has conceived what God has prepared for those who love him"* (1 Cor. 2:9), and *"I consider that our present sufferings are not worth comparing with the glory that will be revealed in us"* (Rom. 8:18). God is good! He is so good!

Let me say it again: God's goodness does not depend on life's situations or even our response to those situations. Goodness is the very essence of God's nature. It's easy to say "God is good" when life is going well and you are enjoying all of His blessings, but can you still say "God is good" when your world seems to be falling apart? Does your view of God's goodness change when your happiness is gone? The reality of life in a sinful world is that there is a mixture of good and bad, of sunshine and rain, of happiness and sadness. But God is unchanging; He is *the same yesterday and today and forever"* (Heb. 13:8); He is *"the Father of the heavenly lights, who does not change like shifting shadows"* (Jas. 1:17b). Psalm 34:8 says, *"Taste and see that the Lord is good; blessed is the man who takes refuge in him."* If God was good then, He is good now, and He is good all the time because He never changes.

The world is a fallen place where sinful people live and where bad things happen, but that does not mean that God does not care. He cared enough to send His only Son, who was without sin, to take the punishment for our sins in our place, so that we could be forgiven and become children of God. And don't think for a minute that God does not know what it is like to suffer. Jesus suffered ridicule and hatred. He suffered a cruel beating and the agony of having nails driven through His hands and feet and hung on a wooden cross in agony to die a slow death. God, His Father, suffered the pain of watching His Son die. The Bible says that Jesus was a *"man of sorrows, and familiar with suffering"* (Is. 53:3b). Whatever might be happening in your life

Does your view of God's goodness change when your happiness is gone?

right now, no matter how bad or painful it is, the Lord knows what you're going through, and He cares. That's why 1 Peter 5:7 says, *"Cast all your anxiety on him because he cares for you."*

Someone once said that trials and sufferings in life either make you bitter or they make you better. The choice is yours. You may not be able to do very much about bad things that happen to you in life, but you can choose whether you will allow them to break you in bitterness or build you to be better. I remember going through many extremely scary and painful procedures in the hospital… the surgeries, rehabilitation, episodes of rejection, needles, IVs, x-rays—too many treatments to mention, all trying to keep my frail body alive. But while in the hospital, no matter how bad my situation was, there always seemed to be someone who was suffering more, with more pain, more procedures, and in some cases, had to face a painful death, at an even younger age.

So in this perspective, I was able to find thankfulness and realize that I am a winner. Remember, no matter how desperate your situation, you can always find someone with a situation even more desperate. This principle is not just for the weak and weary. On the other side of life's coin are those who are very healthy, rich, and prosperous, but no matter how much you have, there always seems to be someone who has more. You break a record and soon someone comes along and breaks your record. You get a big raise at your job and someone else gets an even bigger raise. You buy a big house and your neighbor builds an even bigger house. The top is never the top. There is always someone higher, someone bigger, and someone better.

As is the bottom. No matter how bad your situation, there is always someone in the midst of an even more desperate situation. You will never be at the very top and you will never be at the very bottom. The gap between the two can only be navigated with a heart of thankfulness and gratefulness that humbles us in the good and gives us strength in the bad.

If you look for God in the midst of your painful circumstances, you will find Him right beside you, hurting along with you, and longing to give you peace and comfort. One of my favorite sayings, which I had hanging on my bedroom wall, says: "God is WITH you, Jesus is IN you, and all of Heaven's angels are on your side." I also had a copy of my favorite painting beside my bed. It was the portrait entitled Jesus the Surgeon. It is a vivid picture of Jesus guiding the hands of a surgeon while he was at work. I took comfort in knowing that through all the procedures and the numerous times I was sedated, Jesus was still ultimately in control of what was happening to my body. I had dedicated my body to the Lord and I knew it belonged to Him. Many times, when I was facing pain or uncertainty, when I did not know what was going to happen or whether I was going to live or die, I found strength in Jeremiah 29:11, one of my favorite verses: *"For I know the plans I have for you,' declares the LORD, 'plans to prosper you and not to harm you, plans to give you hope and a future.'"* Even though I have departed my earthly life, what the world calls death was what I call "the grand prize." I was set free from all of my hurt, pain, and affliction. I now dance in wholeness with my heavenly Father. I am prospering more now than I ever dreamed, with a hope brighter than all the stars in the universe combined, and with a future as fast as eternity. Once again, death ZERO, Austin won.

Take it from me: God is good!

CHAPTER 4

TRANSITION TO HEAVEN

In today's day and age many find it hard to even believe that there is a heaven, let alone a hell. With all of the things that are happening in society, we have almost talked ourselves out of the fact that God is real, that Jesus is the Son of God, and that heaven really exists.

Just think about it. We have taken prayer out of school. Today many believe that Jesus was just a good man or very popular prophet. The Bible has become nothing more than the world's best-selling history book. We lay claim to Christianity, but it seems that we have lost "true faith."

Many are ashamed and embarrassed to live a "Christ-like" life. We go through all of the motions when we need to, especially on Sunday mornings, but we never really connect with God. The truth is, to be filled with a living faith in God is what makes the eternal a reality. But faith is a hard thing. It is something you can't see and can't feel; you can't touch it or explain it. Seeing is not faith but reasoning. Faith is truly without sight. It is an experience of the heart that bypasses our fleshly knowledge.

The most important thing parents can do for their children is not to prepare them for life on earth, but to prepare them for life in heaven. My parents certainly believed this and put their belief into practice every day for my sisters and me. In every event in life, in every conversation, in everything that happened, good or bad, Mom and Dad taught us to look at the eternal perspective; to look beyond the pain, fear, hurt, anger, or the question "Why?" of the immediate moment to see the greater purposes of God from His viewpoint in eternity. Mom and Dad were convinced that earthly life is a training ground for heaven, and from my new perspective on this side of that divide I see more clearly than ever before how right they were. Mom and Dad always kept eternity in view and taught me to do the same. They had their hands full with all of my sicknesses and surgeries and tests and procedures, but they never forgot what I needed most of all: faith in Jesus. They believed what Charles H. Spurgeon once said: "Our faith is always at its greatest point when we are in the middle of the trial."

Many parents go all out to make sure their kids have all the best things in life but never teach them to love God. They give them all the latest stuff; they teach them to brush their teeth, eat their vegetables, and use good manners when they talk to others; they teach them right from wrong and the benefits of honesty and hard work; they take them to violin lessons and soccer practice. But seldom do they leave room when it comes to matters of faith. Many parents say, "I don't want to force my beliefs upon my children; I'll let them decide for themselves what they want to believe." My dad often says that fathers are responsible to teach and prepare

> *The most important thing parents can do for their children is not to prepare them for life on earth, but to prepare them for life in heaven.*

their children to face the battles of life. Fathers need to begin to step up to the plate and take their roles seriously. So often, fathers take the "easy chair" and leave it up to the church, the school teachers, and even their spouse to be the instructors and to influence their children into becoming who they should be. It needs to begin with the fathers! You may ask, "How can you prepare your children when you don't know exactly what they will face?" It all comes back to what foundation the fathers are building their lives on and if they are equipping their children with a good, strong foundation in the Lord that will be able to weather their storms of life. When a shipbuilder builds a ship, he doesn't build it to keep it on a scaffold or to protect it from the strong winds and hurricanes. No, he builds it strong enough to face even the toughest challenges. The same needs to be for you, as parents, in preparing your children.

History has proven that, as parents, what you put into your children in many cases is what you get out. The Bible says, *"Train up a child in the way he should go, and when he is old he will not depart from it"* (Prov. 22:6 NKJV™).

As children, we will never learn the true basics of faith and we will never experience life in Christ from the world. Each child is a precious gift of God and it is a parent's responsibility to plant the seeds of faith in the tender hearts of his or her children and water and nurture those seeds to maturity.

Nothing is more important in this life than getting prepared for the next one. Nothing! After all, what is our short time on earth compared to eternity? The Bible says that life is *"a vapor that appears for a little time and then vanishes away"* (Jas. 4:14 NKJV™). But it also says that God's "kingdom will never end" (see Luke 1:33). Which do you think is more important, a vapor that is gone in a moment, or a kingdom that will last forever? You are spinning your wheels if you are spending all of your time and energy on this earthly life that passes so quickly and ignoring the eternity that will follow. Jesus said, *"What good is it for a man to gain the whole world, yet forfeit his soul?"* (Mark 8:36).

Let's face it, life on earth is short. I'm not saying that just because mine was less than 17 years. Your age doesn't matter; next to eternity, earthly life is nothing, no matter how long you live. The Bible says that with God a day is as a thousand years, and a thousand years as a day. Doesn't it make more sense to spend time getting ready for a life that never ends rather than get completely caught up in things that are here today and gone tomorrow?

That's what my parents believed, and that's what they lived in front of me all my life, even up to the very day I made the transition from earthly life to heavenly life. My dad taught me many things, but there were three he kept coming back to, three that he kept telling me over and over again until their truth sank deep into my spirit: 1) "I love you," 2) "God loves you," and 3) "God has a special plan for your life." Many people, upon learning the story of my life and the health issues that were a constant part of it, used to tell me how brave I was and how amazed they were that I seemed to take everything in stride. Was I brave? I don't know; maybe I was, sometimes. But there were many, many times when I didn't feel brave. In fact, there were plenty of times when I was downright scared. I was tired of the pain, tired of the needles, tired of being poked and prodded every five minutes, tired of having to give "just one more" blood sample. When I got tired, it was hard to keep my defenses up, and it was when my defenses began to falter that discouragement began to set in. I knew that leads to fear, and I was not going to go there!

There were times I just wanted to scream, "Stop it! I've had enough! *Leave me alone!*" Then there were the times when I began to feel sorry for myself. "This isn't fair! Why does it always have to be me? Why can't I be healthy? Why can't I have a normal life like other kids? God, do You care? Do You even know where I am?" It was at these low times when I was most discouraged that fear forced its way into my mind like an armed intruder and began to fill my head with lies. "You're going to die." "You will never get out of the hospital." "God doesn't care about you; if He did, why would He let you suffer?" But whenever those kinds of thoughts threatened to drown me in despair and fear, Dad's words always came back to me and banished all the lies: "I love you. God loves you. God has a special plan for your life." If I was ever "brave" or "took

> *Dad's words banished all the lies: "I love you. God loves you. God has a special plan for your life."*

everything in stride," it was because I knew I was loved by my earthly dad and mom, and especially by my heavenly Father, whom I knew and trusted would never allow me to go through anything that was not part of His greater plan and who was right there with me in everything I went through.

From the time my sisters and I were very young, Mom and Dad talked to us honestly and openly about the sacredness and fragility of life, the certainty of death, and how important it was to be ready to meet God. As a family, we enjoyed an openness of talking and sharing with one another that I believe was deeper than that of most families. Perhaps this was due at least in part to the ongoing health issues that affected me and my sister Alisha. None of us knew who would be the first in our family to go, or when, but we understood that it could be any one of us at any time, but especially me or Alisha.

Mom and Dad were always close to me, but especially Dad. He stood by me through all the hardest and scariest and most painful experiences of my life. He was always there for me, even throughout my last day on earth. I had gotten pretty sick the night before, and by the following morning was even worse. Dad came over to the top bunk where I lay and gently placed his hand on my head. I loved the feel of my father's touch; it always calmed me down, which helped me feel better.

"How are you feeling, Austin?" he asked softly.

"I feel sick all over," I told him, "and my back really hurts."

I was so sick that I didn't want Dad to leave my side because his presence somehow made it easier for me to put up with the pain. No one knew yet that it was my last day, but that day Dad prayed for me several times throughout the evening. He would get real close to me, cradle my head in his hands, and pray.

"Father, draw us into Your presence. Carry us to Your throne of grace, where we may find mercy to help in time of need. Lord Jesus, let me sit on one side of Your lap and let Austin sit on the other." Then Dad would ask Jesus for healing for each of my bodily organs and every part of my body. "Lord, Austin's back hurts so much; please take away the pain and heal his back. His stomach is so unsettled; please take away the nausea and give him rest. Strengthen the heart beating in his chest and cleanse his blood of whatever is making him sick. You are the Great Physician and we reclaim Austin's healing in Your name."

That's how it would go. One by one, Dad lifted up each of my bodily organs and parts to the Lord and asked for healing. Then he would conclude by thanking God for answering his prayer. As I lay broken, I watched as my father, piece by piece, lifted me up, offering me to my heavenly Father. That was the day of my transition from earth to heaven; from my relationship with my earthly father into the glorious presence of my heavenly Father. My last conscious memory on earth is of my father praying for me. The next thing I knew, I was opening my eyes to gaze at the face of Jesus, smiling at me. Strength and energy and vitality of health as I had never known flowed through me and filled me. I was home at last! And, as they had always been throughout my life, my mom and dad were with me when I made the crossing. They held me close as I stepped across the threshold of physical death to be embraced by the Lord Jesus and filled with His life that has no end. I am now being cradled in my heavenly Father's hands!

Children's relationship with their earthly fathers should be a mirror reflecting the image of their relationship with their heavenly Father. That's the way it was with my dad. Whenever I looked at Dad, I saw a little bit of what God is like. And although I loved being with my earthly dad, and my family, being in the presence of God, my heavenly Father, is so much greater and so much more fulfilling. The most wonderful thing is that I know we will still experience an even more special and close family relationship when the rest of my family gets here. The relationships on earth are just a small glimpse of how wonderful and complete they are in heaven. God gave us these special bonds not just to take them away from us when we get to heaven but to give us a taste of all the glories that await us. And the close relationships here in heaven are all untainted by sin! I get to experience the best of both worlds! Death got a great big ZERO and I have won the race! Nothing on earth can compare to being accepted so completely, being understood so fully, and being loved so deeply!

Start preparing for the transition!

P.S. I know it's hard to squeeze all of this into our small minds. The idea of dying, going to heaven, having eternal life, and being whole and safe in the arms of Jesus for eternity is extremely hard to fathom.

The earthly pain that my dad felt at my death must have been unbearable, but I am sure that his faith and his willingness to see things in an eternal perspective are what give him strength. I can see him now living out his words. As he looks to the sky, he can see me. I am sure he still hurts, but he is not angry. Because of his faith he can see me whole, without pain and in the arms of my heavenly Father. He knows that soon he will see me again. He taught me how to run this race. And for him the pain may never go away, but because of his faith and his strength he continues to run the race, knowing that his hope of glory is the big picture and eternal perspective.

Run, Dad, run hard. I love you. See you soon...

CHAPTER 5

WHO DO YOU THINK YOU ARE?

I'm going to switch gears here and talk about something that may seem a little off-topic. Growing up is tough in today's world, and may be tougher than ever before, even for young people like me and my sisters who were born into a warm and loving home to parents who loved the Lord and taught us to do the same. Because we were home-schooled, we may have been sheltered from many of the pressures and temptations faced by most children in a formal school setting, whether public or private, but that does not mean we were isolated from problems. We had plenty of social and recreational contact with other families and with other children our age, so we were not naive about many of the challenges they faced, even if they did not directly affect our family.

I could easily write an entire book just on the challenges faced by young people growing up in American society today. The list of possible topics is almost endless: smoking, drinking, sex, drugs, peer pressure, school violence, street violence, gangs, cheating, pornography (especially on the Internet), wild partying, single-parent households, and physical, psychological, or sexual abuse at home…well, I think you get the idea. But right now I want to focus on one particular issue, a problem that affects nearly everyone in one way or another, and, although it has been around a long time, has only in the last few years begun to receive nationwide attention as an increasing problem that needs to be dealt with. I'm talking about bullying.

Bullying has been around as long as people have been gathering in social groups (and that's a long, long time!). I guess you could say that Cain was the world's first bully, who took out his anger at God by murdering his brother Abel (see Genesis 4). Since God was too big for Cain to handle, he chose a smaller victim who was close at hand. That's the way it is with bullies: they never pick on somebody their own size. They always choose somebody who is smaller, weaker, and easily intimidated. Goliath is another example. This Philistine giant bullied the entire army of Israel, including King Saul, challenging them to send just one soldier to meet him in face-to-face combat (see 1 Samuel 17). In typical bully fashion, he knew that his great size and experience as a warrior gave him a lopsided advantage...until a young shepherd named David stepped forward and in the power of God put Goliath in his place.

Unless you are one of the few fortunate enough to avoid either one, you fall into one of two categories: the bully or the bullied. If you fit into the second group, don't worry; you are not alone!

Bullying takes many forms and is not limited to the school environment. It occurs at home, in the workplace, in public and social gatherings, and even, sad to say, in church. In other words, bullying can be found wherever you find people. And while most people probably still think of bullying as involving physical threats, intimidation, and violence, such as stealing a kid's lunch money, tripping him in the hallway, or taking him behind the school building and beating him up, bullying also takes nonphysical forms, such as teasing, mockery, derisive laughter, and making fun. In fact, it seems that these verbal forms of bullying have taken a sharp increase in recent years, particularly with young people's widespread access to the Internet. Don't you remember the story from a few years ago of a junior high student who killed herself because of relentless verbal bullying other students subjected her to on Facebook? That may be an extreme example, but it is no less tragic for being so and it illustrates how bullying has come into the national limelight. Statistics show that three out of four children, between the ages of 8 and 11, have been bullied. And 80% of teenagers have had some sort of bullying experience.

There was a time in years past (or so I was told) when bullying was looked on as unfortunate but not considered a serious problem. Many people, including many adults, dismissed it by saying, "Well, that's just how it is being a kid. Bullying is just part of growing up." I wonder how many folks who thought that way ever bothered to ask a bully's victim how he or she felt about it! If you have ever been victimized by a bully, I'm sure you can recall how it felt like you were in a no-win situation, feeling that you had nowhere to turn.

If you did nothing or said nothing about the bullying, it would continue. If you spoke up and told someone, however, such as a teacher or a parent, you would be called a "squealer" or a "tattletale," and even students who had been friendly to you before would lose respect for you and might even start bullying you themselves.

Whoever originated the saying, "Sticks and stones may break my bones, but words can never hurt me," got it completely wrong.

Today, if anything, bullying is worse than it used to be, particularly the verbal kind. Verbal bullying is even more serious than the physical variety because while a physical beating may be painful for several minutes or several hours, verbal bullying can inflict emotional and psychological wounds that hurt for a lifetime. Whoever originated the saying, "Sticks and stones may break my bones, but words can never hurt me," got it completely wrong. Unkind words and verbal abuse can hurt deeply and can even be deadly, as I mentioned with the Facebook example.

I was not a stranger to bullying. Although I never had much trouble from physical bullying, verbal bullying was a different story. When I played Little League baseball, I was completely bald due to a condition known as Alopecia Universalis. For several years I had no hair at all on my body, not even eyebrows or eyelashes. For the most part, people were understanding and kind to me in spite of my condition, but there were also some, mostly other children, who were insensitive or even cruel, openly staring at me and making hurtful comments. More than once I had my feelings hurt when a fellow team member or member of another team said to me, "I don't like you because you don't have any hair!" or "I don't want to play with you because you look funny!" I have since learned that people of all ages often ridicule something they don't understand, or something that makes them feel afraid, or someone who seems very different from them. But as a young boy I did not understand that, and so those unkind comments cut me deeply. Fortunately, I had two really great things going for me at that time. First, there were my mom and dad, who loved me, made me feel secure in their love, and taught me to dismiss the negative and focus on the positive. Then there was my best friend,

Alan, who always accepted me just the way I was. He and I had some great times together, and it was much easier for me to forget about the negative comments others had said about me. The older I got, the less bothered I was at negative words or actions toward me because I knew I was loved and accepted fully by those closest to me.

My sister Alisha probably struggled more than I did with verbal bullying, especially with remarks about her skin and allergy issues. Some of her so-called "friends" made cutting comments that hurt her deeply, like, "I don't like you because of your skin," or "I am not going to play with you anymore because I am afraid that I will get what you have," or "You don't look very nice because of that stuff on your skin." Alisha already felt self-conscious enough about the painful allergic reactions and severe rashes that discolored and disfigured her skin; hurtful comments such as these only made her feel worse about herself. The bullying Alisha received bothered me more than my own because I loved my sister and hated to see her hurt.

Alisha struggled for a long time with accepting herself. Sometimes she got so discouraged that she said, "I hate my skin!" Mom and Dad were always telling Alisha how beautiful she was both inside and out, but it took her a while to believe it herself. They assured her that the children who made those comments did not realize how much they were hurting her. They encouraged her to thank God for her skin and to list all the ways that her skin was beneficial to her. This was a big help to her in learning to accept herself the way God made her. Mom and Dad were always very wise in this regard, in knowing how to help us see our lives and our particular situation from a different perspective, not the perspective of the world, but the perspective of heaven. They helped us learn to love others as God loves and to realize that everyone is "different" and "special" in his or her own way.

One of the most important things that parents can do to protect their children is to have open and direct conversations with them so they feel safe enough to share their hearts and struggles with you. Also, look for other signs that may alert you that there is a problem. You may see unexplained bruises, torn clothes or belongings, mood swings, or ongoing physical symptoms.

You may struggle all of your life with people who don't treat you like you think they should. There are so many ways that people can hurt you and the enemy wants to destroy you through these events. There are some foundational concepts that will also help you to understand why these things are happening. First of all, it helps to realize that we are created in three different parts: our spirit, our soul, and our body. I listed them in the order of importance. Most of the time, we see ourselves as being a body and possessing a soul and a spirit. It is very important for us to understand that the real person that we are is our spirit. God's goal for us is for us to be mighty in spirit. When you are mistreated or abused, it is crucial that you understand that although your body may have been damaged, you can choose whether or not if your soul and spirit will also be damaged. You can allow God to help your spirit to grow stronger because of it or you can become angry and bitter and allow the offender to keep controlling your life in this way.

If you are being verbally abused, you can neutralize the venom by forgiving your offender and by speaking words of blessing to him or her. I know, this sounds rather far out…but try it! It really does work. You will notice that God will do a great work in your heart and the negative words will not affect you in the ways they once did.

Another valuable thing to do is to know who you are in Christ. If you realize that you are a spirit (with an eternal soul and a physical body) that is created in God's own image and that you are very valuable and beautiful in His sight, you will then be better equipped to refute the lies that are being sent your way. If you have dedicated your body to the Lord, then you will also realize that what is happening to your body is also being done to Him. He is suffering along with you, and He has promised that vengeance belongs to Him and He will repay for the wrong that was done to you.

I think it also helps us to understand who we are when we understand how God created us with the "longings" that we have in our hearts. Don't you find yourself searching for significance, for love, for feeling like you really want to belong somewhere or to someone? At times, these "longings for more" turn people into becoming loud and self-centered as they attempt to draw attention to themselves. Maybe you are seeking for significance by climbing the ladder of success in your job or by looking to material things to fill that empty spot in your heart. You may even be looking to good things like relationships to satisfy the deep longing that you feel. Although these can all bring a sense of fulfillment, especially when God is in the center of those relationships, you will soon realize that there is still a longing—a yearning—that is never quite satisfied. This is because God created each of us with a "God-shaped" vacuum that will never be completely filled until we are face to face with Jesus. Not until you get to heaven will you have all of your longings met. Don't look to any other person, object, or relationship to

Only until you get to heaven will you have all of your longings met.

meet them. God uniquely created you in this way so that you would have a desire for Him and for heaven. And, believe me, you will never be disappointed! You will then feel like the greatest winner ever!

Now, I have shared a lot about identifying abusive situations, realizing our true value, and using that value as a strength to overcome these situations. Before I close this chapter, I would like to share just a little bit to those who find themselves in situations where they are abusive and destructive to others.

"Bully" is a word that we use to describe a person who finds pleasure in hurting someone whom he or she feels has lesser value than him or herself. What is interesting is that "bullies" are disguised in all kinds of packages. They are not always just big, tough guys, picking on the little guy. They are human—body, soul, and spirit—just like everyone else. Some are very big and strong, some very pretty, and some are very smart and witty. These are God-given strengths, but we must choose how we want to use these strengths. We can use them to help others or we can use them as a weapon that hurts others. And in many cases, a person who inflicts pain on another has a history of being bullied or abused—either physically, verbally, or mentally—by someone in his or her life. Hurt breeds hurt. The only answer is to determine in your heart to break the cycle. Using your strengths to uplift and protect others around you is ultimately the first step to your own personal healing. Learning to use your strengths to defend, protect, and build up is what makes a "hero."

I, as well as a lot of my friends, love sports. You have football, baseball, basketball, and soccer. All of us had our favorite athletes. We looked up to them and we respected them for their strength and ability. As strong as these athletes are, it would be very rare to hear of them using their strength to purposely hurt someone else. And not only are they strong in the game, but many also maintain a strong influence in society. They find great pleasure in using their strength to help others. They became very respected heroes to many. So, using your strength to defend instead of hurt, to protect instead of turning away, and to bring peace where there is heartache or chaos is the true measure of a person's integrity and dignity. And that is the mark of a true winner.

CHAPTER 6

LIVING UP TO YOUR FULL POTENTIAL

Have you ever wished you had been born in a different time or place in history? Maybe you read a book or watched a movie that captured your imagination about a faraway place or a long-ago time and you thought, "Wow! I would love to have lived back then!" Or, "I wish I could live in that place!" Sometimes it is fun to imagine what your life might have been like had you been born under different circumstances. I have found, though, that if you do this, it will breed a spirit of discontentment. I would have become very miserable in life if I had focused for a long time on how it could have been.

People used to ask me if I ever regretted the circumstances of my life, that there were some things that other young people my age enjoyed doing that I could not do because of my health issues. I will admit that, yes, sometimes it was hard, but as I mentioned previously, that was the reality of my life—one of those unchangeable factors that I had to accept and learn how to live with. Having never known any other kind of life, I suppose the adjustment was easier for me than for someone who enjoyed complete and vigorous health for a long time only to suddenly lose it. Would I have changed my situation if I could have? Sure, who wouldn't? At the same time, however, I would not trade anything for the life lessons I learned because of my circumstances, especially the intimate and deeply personal way I came to know Christ.

You have to take life as it comes because there is so much of life that you have no control over. For example, you have no control over the time or circumstances into which you are born. You cannot choose the time or the place of your birth, or who your parents are, or your siblings, or whether your family will be rich, poor, or somewhere in between. Your genetic makeup is predetermined from the moment you are conceived. Your DNA is set, and it determines your height, weight, body size and type, your eye and hair color, your IQ, natural talents and abilities, and even what illnesses or other health issues you may or may not be prone to. With so much that you cannot change, the best thing you can do is learn to make the most of the life that God has given you.

I'm talking about quality of life, not quantity. I'm talking about making the days of your life count, not merely counting the days of your life. What good does it do to live 80, 90, or even 100 years and have little or nothing to show for your life? Wouldn't it be better to live for a few years and make a difference than to live for a century and leave no mark? It's not how long you live that matters as much as how well you live. What matters is not how much time you have on earth but what you do with the time you have.

> *Wouldn't it be better to live for a few years and make a difference than to live for a century and leave no mark?*

Life is precious, partly because it is so short, especially compared to eternity. My dad compares the briefness of life as a thought that crosses through our minds. Very quickly it is gone! That little dash between the dates on our tombstones looks so insignificant, but how we live the little dash determines our complete eternal destiny! With life being so short, time really is of the essence. Time is precious because we only go through this life once, and time wasted is gone forever. So how we use our time in this life is very important because a missed opportunity may not come around again. The apostle Paul understood the importance of using our time wisely:

Be very careful, then, how you live—not as unwise but as wise, making the most of every opportunity, because the days are evil (Ephesians 5:15-16).

According to Paul, a life of significance means using your time wisely, and that means making the most of your opportunities. I guess another way to say it would be that a life of significance means living up to your full potential.

No matter who you are, you have the potential for greatness—the same potential that God places within every person. I'm not saying necessarily that you are destined for fame and fortune or world renown—few people are—but that God has equipped you with everything you need to live a life of significance and influence in whatever tiny part of the world He has placed you. God judges greatness by standards different from the world's. The world judges greatness according to money and power and political influence. God, on the other hand, finds greatness in the humble heart of a servant.

One day when the brothers James and John, two of Jesus' disciples, asked Him to promise them the top two positions in His government, the other ten disciples were angry, probably because they each hoped for those same positions for themselves. Jesus saw this as an excellent teaching moment and used it to the fullest.

> *Jesus called them together and said, "You know that the rulers of the Gentiles lord it over them, and their high officials exercise authority over them. Not so with you. Instead, whoever wants to become great among you must be your servant, and whoever wants to be first must be your slave— just as the Son of Man did not come to be served, but to serve, and to give his life as a ransom for many"* (Matthew 20:25-28).

Greatness in God's eyes is found in obedience to Him and in serving others in His name. By this definition, you can be great whoever you are and wherever you are, even if no one outside a small circle of family, friends, and acquaintances ever knows your name. All that is required is for you to submit humbly to the Lord and His plan for your life, tap into the mighty ocean of potential He has placed inside you, and commit yourself to serving God's purpose in your generation. This is exactly what the Bible said about King David of Israel: *"For when David had served God's purpose in his own generation, he fell asleep* [and] *was buried with his fathers..."* (Acts 13:36). The Bible also says that David was a man after God's own heart. Sure, he made mistakes, and plenty of them, just as we all do, but David's life was significant because his heart was committed to God. And your committed heart is all God needs to make your life significant.

> *A significant life does not necessarily mean a long life.*

A significant life does not necessarily mean a long life. Jesus walked the earth for only 33 years, but His life was the most significant of anyone who has ever lived, and the reason is because He was committed to accomplishing the will and purpose of His Father.

My dad reminded me almost daily of God's great love for me and of the eternal purpose He had for my life. He helped me understand that my purpose in life began with consistent obedience in the things that I understood and then to faithfully live that out each day. The purpose of life is not for us to seek pleasure and focus selfishly on doing all the things that we want to do, but about living our lives for the furtherance of God's kingdom; of serving God's purpose in our generation.

Mom and Dad believed in God's eternal purpose for me; neither my ongoing health issues nor the very real possibility that my life would be short made any difference. They taught me that God could use me and that my life could have significance despite the physical frailty of my body and whether I lived many years or few. When I was 15, Dad arranged a special "Calling into Manhood" service for me. He recognized that I was becoming a man and wanted to make sure that I took this calling seriously. My family and friends and a few of Dad's mentors were there. Both of my grandpas took part because Dad wanted them and other people of godly influence to speak into my life—to pronounce blessings on my life—and in this way help mold me into the man God had called me to be.

I remember quoting Matthew chapters 5, 6, and 7 almost word for word. Then each of the godly men present spoke their blessings into my life. To seal this precious commitment service before God, they then anointed me for the "greater works" that Jesus said His followers would do. They wanted me to be able to fulfill all that God desired for my life. I cannot adequately describe the impact this service had on my life. The blessings that were spoken and the anointing that I received that evening imparted to me the unmistakable and unshakable realization that God's hand was upon my life and filled me with the deep desire to prepare myself for God's calling on me, whatever form it took. The grace of God, the faith of these mentors, and their crying out in prayer to God on my behalf touched me in a way that nothing else ever had.

My earthly life ended less than a year later. Does that mean my "Calling into Manhood" service was a waste of time? Does it mean that the blessings spoken over me, and the anointing I received, were meaningless? Absolutely not! Think about it. You are reading this book, aren't you? God does not measure by our standards or follow our timetable. Living up to our full potential means making the most of every day and every opportunity to live for the glory of God, no matter how many days, or how few, God grants us on earth. In the weeks and months following this service, I experienced a deeper faith and a greater sense of peace in the Lord than ever before. Many people, both at the hospitals and at our various ministry services, were very open to hear my story and I was blessed to see many of them drawn to the Lord because of it. Others were drawn to the Lord even while I was on my deathbed in the hospital and wasn't even breathing on my own. This is because I was open to God using me however He chose to. My parents prayed many times that God would use each of us children to draw others unto the Lord and to make us mighty in spirit. They dedicated us to God so we were His to use for His honor and glory. He answered their prayers regarding my life. However, it wasn't the life that they had envisioned. When I was an infant, my mom prayed that I would be a missionary or an evangelist who would touch many people's lives. Because I followed God's purpose, God is able to do that through me.

Each of us has a specific work from God that He wants us to do. I did, and so do you. It doesn't matter how old you are, or where you are in life, or what restrictions or limitations or weaknesses you have to deal with. If you are willing, and if your heart is committed to the Lord, He can and will use you right where you are to bless others and bring glory to His name. Don't let lack of faith or fear of failure keep you from living up to your full potential. Commit your way to the Lord and set yourself to make the most of the opportunities He gives you every day.

I remember at my funeral there were those who said, "He just couldn't take it anymore." Or, "He finally lost the battle." But the truth is that death has no grip on me. Instead of saying that I died, I like to say that I have been set free. And trust me, I have not been laid to rest. I am completely whole. I run, I dance, I jump, and sometimes I believe I could fly! I am at peace, totally free. I won the battle and death got nothing more than the big "goose egg": a giant zero. Living up to your potential may sometimes seem impossible. You hear the negative words all around you. That's when you take your eyes off of the circumstances, focus on the goal, and run, run, run like the wind with a deaf ear to anything that stands between you and your true God-given potential.

Shut your eyes for a moment and see it, feel it, taste it, then live it, and, without fear, run toward the prize. Losing is not an option. Remember, everyone was born with a God-given potential. It is in you. It is a part of every fiber in your being. It is in your DNA. Let the winner in you take over. Run the race. Run it hard. And live up to your potential.

CHAPTER 7

THE MEASURE OF A MAN

In the previous chapter I talked about my "Coming into Manhood" ceremony, so I think now is a good time for me to talk a little bit about what I think it means to be a man. I know, I know, someone is thinking right about now, "But, Austin, how can you talk about what it means to be a man when you never made it to manhood?" That's true; I was not officially an adult when I was "set free." Legally, I was still a minor. But I think I know something about manhood because I saw it modeled consistently by my dad, my grandpas, and other significant men in my life. I saw true manhood in these men in the way they openly and unashamedly demonstrated their love for God and walked faithfully in obedience to Him. I saw it in my dad, particularly in the way he always showed love, honor, and respect for my mom, my sisters, and me. I saw it in the way he always directed our minds and hearts to the Lord no matter what was happening in our lives at the time. Whether in good times or bad, he always reminded us to take it to the Lord, and then he led the way. Dad led by word and example, and he was always right there by my side through all the most difficult, unpleasant, and painful experiences I went through. I learned so much about manhood from watching my dad that even when I was 16 and still legally a minor, I felt that I had the mind and heart of a man.

So what is the measure of a man? Love for God and family (in that order), respect and honor for wife and children, spiritual leadership in the home, and faithfulness to the Lord in daily life. But that's not all. Dad also taught me the difference between the behavior of a man and that of a child. Becoming a man means putting away childish thoughts and attitudes and taking up the mantle of maturity and responsibility that characterizes a true man. The apostle Paul described it this way:

> *When I was a child, I talked like a child, I thought like a child, I reasoned like a child. When I became a man, I put childish ways behind me* (1 Corinthians 13:11).

Children believe that anything is possible; they don't understand the difference between fantasy and reality. (Unfortunately, there are many "grown-ups" who have the same problem!) One aspect of true manhood is recognizing and accepting the realities of life, particularly the fact that there are some things we cannot change, no matter how much we might like to. Dad taught me that there are ten basic "unchangeables" in life that we must accept and work with if we are to become mature adults:

1. Our parents
2. Our brothers and/or sisters
3. Birth and place of birth
4. Our birth order in the family
5. Our unique makeup
6. The time in history when we were born
7. Our gender
8. Our physical features and mental capacity
9. The fact that we are aging
10. The time of our death.[1]

All of these are defining characteristics for us that were set before we were ever born. Every one of us is,

---

1. These ten "unchangeables" come from the Institute in Basic Life Principles. Used by permission.

without exception, as God made us. We all possess certain God-given traits and characteristics of body, mind, and spirit that, when combined, make each one of us a totally unique individual. We may not like some of our personal traits, such as our hair color or our height or our weight or the fact that we have freckles or that we have allergies or other health challenges, but even those undesired characteristics contribute to make us who we are. So if there are parts of you that you don't like, remember this: God created you just the way you are, and the Bible says that God declared everything He created to be good! He loves you just the way He made you, and He thinks you are the greatest! Your self-worth is not determined by either the beauty or the blemishes of your physical features or your character, but by the fact that you are a precious and unique individual created in the image of God. Part of mature manhood (and womanhood, for that matter) is accepting yourself the way God made you

> *Part of mature manhood is accepting yourself the way God made you.*

and embracing your uniqueness as God's personal stamp of approval and creativity upon you. Take up all the traits and characteristics that make you you, and think of them as God's marks of ownership on your life.

Strange as it may sound, I regard the frailty of my physical body on earth as some of my marks of God's ownership. All of that was part of what made me uniquely me. Another mark of ownership was when for many years I had no hair. I mentioned earlier that I developed a condition called Alopecia Universalis, which left me completely bald, including eyebrows and eyelashes. At first, I was bothered and felt self-conscious at the rude stares I received in many places where we went. Eventually, as with everything else, I got used to the stares and the comments, so they didn't bother me as much. Besides, there were plenty of people, including some good friends my age, who accepted me for who I was and to whom my strange appearance did not matter.

As I got a little older and had been without hair for several years, my parents asked me if I would like to try wearing a wig whenever we went out in public. I said that was okay, so they shopped around to find a wig that suited me. The idea was fine, but the problem was that I was still young enough not to fully understand that the purpose of the wig was to give me a more normal appearance so that people would stop staring at me. I thought of it more as something that I would wear like a hat; if it felt hot, I simply took it off! Needless to say, Mom was appalled the first time I did that! Pulling my wig off drew more attention than if I had simply gone without it. By that time, however, it just didn't matter to me that I was out in public. Mom soon helped me understand that I didn't want to get that kind of attention.

The older I got, and the more secure I became in the knowledge of my family's love for me as well as God's love for me, I became less and less concerned about what other people thought of me. If someone didn't accept me for who I was, I just shrugged it off and thought about the friends I did have who loved and accepted me unconditionally. Mom and Dad also taught me that I was special just the way God had created me. I was unique, and all those things that characterized my uniqueness— surviving two heart transplants, surviving two kinds of cancer, and those years of baldness—were special marks of God's ownership on me.

There was one mark of God's ownership in my life that was greater than all the others, a mark that is shared by all of the children of God: the presence of the Holy Spirit. When we become Christians, God marks us with His Holy Spirit as proof that we belong to Him. The apostle Paul refers to it as a "deposit":

> *Now it is God who makes both us and you stand firm in Christ. He anointed us, set his seal of ownership on us, and put his Spirit in our hearts as a deposit, guaranteeing what is to come* (2 Corinthians 1:21-22).

The Holy Spirit is God's guarantee given to believers as assurance that all His promises will come true, especially His promise of eternal life through Jesus Christ. And you can take it from me: that promise is true! Where I once knew eternal life in Christ by faith, seeing a "poor reflection as in a mirror," I now see "face to face." Where once I knew "in part," I now know "fully, even as I am fully known" (1 Cor 13:12). If you are a believer in Christ, you bear the mark of God's ownership—the Holy Spirit—and everything that is true for me now will also be true for you someday.

When you belong to God—when His mark of ownership is upon you—you should be able to see and experience His hand on your life. I can think of many such times: the time during my cancer when I was in constant and severe stomach pain and felt an invisible hand touch my stomach and take the pain away; the time when Dad and I went into a store to look at pocket knives, and I did not have enough money to buy one, but a complete stranger, in his kindness, bought me not one, but two pocket knives; the time when I was in the hospital on my 16th birthday waiting for my second heart transplant, and another complete stranger, a businessman, bought me the one gift I wanted most of all, a brand-new MacBook. (What an amazing gift!) These are just a few examples.

As these examples show, God's hand on your life does not always mean something miraculous; quite often His hand is revealed in very ordinary things like a pocket knife, or a MacBook, or even a hunting trip. My maternal grandpa is an avid hunter, and from a very young age I enjoyed watching his hunting videos. Over the years I learned the techniques of hunting and even went through some hunter's safety courses. It all paid off when I had the chance to go on a very special hunting trip sponsored by an organization that plans such trips especially for boys who have cancer or who have faced cancer. My dad and I joined a group of others on a five-day hunting excursion to the Outer Banks of North Carolina. One of our companions on the trip and who became one of my hunting buddies was Will Graham, the son of Franklin Graham, who operates the Samaritan's Purse ministry, and the grandson of Billy Graham, the evangelist. Since I always admired Billy Graham, I thought it was really neat to spend some time with his grandson.

That five-day trip was the hunt of my life! God blessed me with not only a black bear but also two bobcats and a swan! Everybody on the trip was excited for me because bobcats were a rare find in that area, especially two of them during one trip! I could not take any credit for finding these animals. Although I may have known the proper strategies for "bagging" these trophies because of the training I had received, I am convinced it was God who brought these animals across my path.

The true measure of a man, and especially a man of God, has nothing to do with being "macho," or "never letting them see you sweat," or being too tough to show your emotions. True manhood does not mean always insisting on doing things your own way, or being so self-reliant that you don't have to depend on anyone else. On the contrary, true biblical manhood means just the opposite: it means doing things God's way and acknowledging that you are totally dependent upon Him. Even Jesus Himself, the greatest model of true manhood who ever walked the earth, relied completely on His heavenly Father. Biblical manhood means that you never boast about yourself or your possessions or your accomplishments; you boast only in the Lord:

> *This is what the LORD says: "Let not the wise man boast of his wisdom or the strong man boast of his strength or the rich man boast of his riches, but let him who boasts boast about this: that he understands and knows me, that I am the LORD, who exercises kindness, justice and righteousness on earth, for in these I delight," declares the LORD* (Jeremiah 9:23-24).

The measure of a man of God is that he lives for tomorrow, for eternity, even as he celebrates the life God gives him each day. It is so easy to get caught up in the negative experiences and circumstances of life that you can forget about all the blessings and other good things that make life enjoyable. Get in the habit daily of looking around you for opportunities to celebrate life. Instead of fretting over what you cannot do, whether because of illness or some other limitation, celebrate the things you can do. As someone has said, learn to eliminate the negative and accentuate the positive.

Learn to savor the personal journey that God has placed you on. Instead of focusing on the emptiness you feel over the death of a loved one, thank God for all the wonderful years He blessed you with that loved one's presence and cherish all the precious memories you have of that person—all the fun times and laughter you shared. If you are burdened with tremendous stress or tension at work, thank God that you have a job and that He is providing for you and your family. If you feel overwhelmed by household clutter and mountains of laundry and dirty dishes, thank God that you are not alone in the world but have loved

> *The measure of a man of God is that he lives for tomorrow, for eternity, even as he celebrates the life God gives him each day.*

ones close to you who are causing the clutter and creating those mountains. If you or a loved one is diagnosed with cancer or another very serious illness, thank God for the lessons you will learn through this experience, the compassion that will grow in you for others going through similar situations, and for the opportunity this experience will give you to draw close to God. I could go on, but I think you get the idea.

The measure of a man is recognizing that the purpose of life in this world is to prepare for life in the world to come, living accordingly, and doing everything he can to help friends, family, and any others within his reach to prepare for the same. Life in this world is temporary. These bodies of flesh, no matter how strong or how frail, are going to die and decay. Don't trust in yourself or in the things of this world; instead, prepare yourself to be *"clothed with* [your] *heavenly dwelling,"* as Paul states it so well:

> *Now we know that if the earthly tent we live in is destroyed, we have a building from God, an eternal house in heaven, not built by human hands. Meanwhile we groan, longing to be clothed with our heavenly dwelling, because when we are clothed, we*

will not be found naked. For while we are in this tent,
we groan and are burdened, because we do not wish
to be unclothed but to be clothed with our heavenly
dwelling, so that what is mortal may be swallowed
up by life. Now it is God who has made us for this
very purpose and has given us the Spirit as a deposit,
guaranteeing what is to come (2 Corinthians 5:1-5).

Love for God; love for family; respect and honor for all; spiritual leadership in the home; faithfulness to the Lord in daily life; maturity; responsibility; recognizing the marks of God's ownership; committed to God's way; totally dependent upon God; living for eternity; savoring life's journey; preparing for the life to come—these are all the attributes of the measure of a man.

No matter how difficult the situation in your life might be, allowing these attributes to be a daily part of your life is what fuels the heart of a winner.

How do you measure up?

CHAPTER 8

IS YOUR CONSCIENCE CLEAR?

All this talk about the measure of a man brings to my mind a related topic that I think is important enough to talk about separately: maintaining a clear conscience. Mature and responsible men and women of God always seek to keep "short accounts" both with God and with other people. They make every effort, as far as it is in their power, to leave no issue unresolved that stands between them and someone else, especially if they themselves have caused the problem.

"What's the big deal?" you might ask. "People make mistakes. After all, nobody's perfect. We can't expect to get along with everybody all the time. Is somebody mad at you? Don't worry about it; he'll get over it."

Are you sure he or she will "get over it"? How do you know? What you see as no "big deal" may be a very *big* deal to somebody else. Are you willing to risk the loss of a relationship over a simple misunderstanding? Misunderstandings have led to more disputes and conflicts between people than any other single cause. Marriages have been destroyed, friendships have been broken, and wars have been fought because people misunderstood each other and failed to resolve the problem before it got out of hand. It's true: misunderstandings do happen and we all make mistakes because we are human. That's not the problem. The problem comes in ignoring the misunderstanding and assuming it will blow over. It is dangerous to assume everything is okay even if it appears to be. Someone may be nursing anger or hurt or resentment even if he or she doesn't say anything. It's much better to clear the air and resolve the issue quickly than risk having it unexpectedly blow up later.

I think there are two main reasons why people tend to ignore misunderstandings rather than deal with them: pride and fear. First, we are too proud to admit that we may have made a mistake or hurt someone with our rash or thoughtless words. After all, it is so much easier to try to justify ourselves by saying, "Well, after all, I'm only human," than it is to go to the other person and say, "I'm sorry."

A second reason why we often fail to deal with misunderstanding is fear of confrontation. After all, who wants to revisit a situation or subject that has already caused hurt and discomfort on both sides? We rationalize our inaction by saying, "If I go to him/her about this, I will only make things worse." Maybe confronting the issue with the other person involved will make the situation worse, at least in the short run, but that is no excuse for ignoring it. Doing nothing at all could be even more devastating.

It's like dealing with a serious illness: sometimes the road to healing starts with more pain rather than less. If you have cancer, for example, you can't afford to ignore it, even if at first it does not cause you any pain or discomfort. Ignoring it will only make it worse. Treatment of your cancer, however, while perhaps healing you in the long run, may make you extremely uncomfortable in the short run. When I was battling cancer at the age of six and seven, I went through repeated six-week cycles of chemotherapy: one week in the hospital for treatment followed by five weeks at home. That may sound like an easy regimen, but as I mentioned in an earlier chapter, my chemotherapy treatments left me so completely drained and weakened physically that it took every day of the following five weeks in the hospital to get my white counts up and to rebuild my strength enough to endure the next treatment. It was a rough time not only for me, but also for my family, and especially Mom and Dad. In the long run, though, chemotherapy helped send my cancer into remission. So in one sense at least, I had to get worse before I could get better. It's the same way with "sick" relationships: sometimes you have to endure the short-term pain of confrontation in order to enjoy the long-term fruits of reconciliation. As any athlete in training knows: no pain, no gain.

> *Sometimes the road to healing starts with more pain rather than less.*

Another excuse people use for not dealing with misunderstanding or conflict is, "He/she is just as much at fault as I am. Why should I be the one to make the first move?" You know what I say to that? *It doesn't matter whose fault it is!* What's more important: fixing blame, or preserving a relationship? You can't afford to wait for the other person to make the first move; you may be waiting a long time, while in the meantime resentment continues to fester like an untreated wound. Even though you cannot control someone else's words or actions, you can control what you say or do. Paul said, *"If it is possible, as far as it depends on you, live at peace with everyone"* (Rom. 12:18). "As far as it depends on you..." means doing whatever you have to do on your part to live at peace with everyone, even those you are in conflict with. It means, if necessary, swallowing your pride and putting the good of others ahead of your own. Again, in Paul's words, *"Nobody should seek his own good, but the good of others"* (1 Cor. 10:24) and *"Do nothing out of selfish ambition or vain conceit, but in humility consider others better than yourselves. Each of you should look not only to your own interests, but also to the interests of others"* (Phil. 2:3-4).

Even more important is the fact that living in conflict with another person without doing everything reasonable within your power to resolve that conflict hinders your relationship with God. You cannot be right with God without being right with other people as far as it depends on you. Jesus made this clear when He said, *"Therefore, if you are offering your gift at the altar and there remember that your brother has something against you, leave your gift there in front of the altar. First go and be reconciled to your brother; then come and offer your gift"* (Matt. 5:23-24). There's nothing here about waiting for the other person to come to you. Jesus said that if you know of ("remember") a conflict between you and another person, it is your responsibility to take the initiative to resolve that conflict and to do it right away.

But what does all this have to do with keeping a clear conscience? For one thing, if you fail or refuse to do something you know you should do, you will end up with a feeling of guilt, which will cloud your conscience. To put it another way, "Anyone, then, who knows the good he ought to do and doesn't do it, sins" (Jas. 4:17). You may not consciously recognize it as guilt, but deep inside you will know that something is not right, that something in your life is out of sync. You will find yourself at odds with God and with other people but won't understand why. Guilt is a product of sin, and sin drives a wedge between you and God, making it impossible for you to approach the heavenly Father on a heart level. Guilt makes you aware of your sin, and that awareness produces shame. Together, guilt and shame make you want to avoid God just as Adam and Eve did when they tried to hide from God in the Garden of Eden.

A guilty conscience puts more people into psychiatric wards and mental hospitals than any other single cause. God created us as social creatures who thrive in an atmosphere of fellowship and harmony, and the absence of those elements affects us physically, emotionally, and spiritually. Some people become so overwhelmed by feelings of guilt and shame that they suffer a mental or emotional breakdown that makes them unable to function in normal society. For others, their guilty conscience creates feelings of self-hatred and worthlessness that drive them to abusive language and behavior toward others as well as self-destructive tendencies. Subconsciously, they feel that they are so "bad" that they don't deserve to be happy and set out to destroy everything they hold dear.

So what about you? Is your conscience clear? As far as it depends on you, are you at peace with everyone you know? Is there any wrong you need to make right, any person to whom you need to go for forgiveness, any mistake you need to own up to, any restitution you need to make to someone you have wronged, any sin you need to confess to God? If any of these apply to you, don't delay; deal with it right away. The longer you wait, the easier it will be to just let the issue slide and the greater the damage to your own spirit, not to mention your relationship with the other person.

So what about you? Is your conscience clear?

Dealing with conflict or misunderstanding quickly is not just a good idea; it is a biblical command: *"In your anger do not sin': Do not let the sun go down while you are still angry, and do not give the devil a foothold"* (Eph. 4:26-27). It is important to God and to your spiritual welfare that you keep "short accounts" with friends, family, and anyone else you have dealings with on a frequent basis. If you know that a conflict exists between you and another person, go to that person as soon as you can and seek resolution. As I said before, it doesn't matter who is to blame for the conflict. If you are angry with another person, go to that person; if that person is angry with you, go to that person. Take the initiative, whether or not you think you are to blame.

I learned early on in life the importance of keeping "short accounts," especially with my family. There were times when I was angry or had some kind of issue with one of my sisters, or with Mom or Dad, or vice versa, and it bothered me so much that I could not go to sleep at night without clearing the air first. I would go to whoever I had wronged and try to make things right. In fact, more times than I care to remember I went to someone in my family before bed to apologize for my bad attitude or for something unkind or hurtful I had said that day. It wasn't always easy, particularly at first, but once I discovered the peace and joy that comes with a clear conscience, I knew that I did not want to live any other way.

The shortness of my own life on earth is a good illustration of another reason why it is important to keep short accounts: you never know when your final opportunity for reconciliation will come. None of us knows the day of our own death, much less that of someone else. Deal with your issue today, for you might not have tomorrow. Don't put yourself in the position of having to say with regret someday, "I never told her how sorry I was," or "I wish he knew that I was no longer mad at him." Remember, sin and a guilty conscience are a breeding ground for fear. And fear breeds death…not only physical death, but also death to your hopes and dreams.

My conscience is clear today that at the time of my passing there was nothing between me and any member of my family that was not made right. We all kept short accounts with each other, which is why our family was so happy, so harmonious, and so full of joy even in spite of the challenges we faced with Alisha's and my health issues.

Psalm 133:1 says, *"How good and pleasant it is when brothers live together in unity."* Jesus said, *"Blessed are the peacemakers, for they will be called sons of God"* (Matt. 5:9). A clear conscience is a good thing, a pleasant thing, a blessed thing. No issue or disagreement is worth ruining a good relationship. Where do you stand? Is your conscience clear?

I am sure you know what I am about to say, but I will say it anyway. Your conscience can work for you or against you. Maintaining a clear conscience assures you that you are running the winner's race.

CHAPTER 9

THE UNEXPLAINABLE EXPERIENCE OF FAITH

I remember when I was little and playing with my sisters or some of my other friends and how we would sometimes ask each other, "What do you want to be when you grow up?" One of us would say, "I want to be a fireman!" "I want to be a policeman!" Somebody else would say, "I want to be a teacher," or "I want to be an astronaut." As a child, it is a lot of fun to dream about what you might want to do with your life; about what job or career or profession you would like to have. These are important questions, but as you get older you realize that there is more involved than just a career choice because some of the most important things in life can't be that clearly defined. So let me ask you, what do you want to be when you "grow up"? Wealthy? Powerful? Successful? Healthy? Happy? All of the above?

To put the question in more grown-up terms, what do you want out of life? Where do you want life to take you? How are you going to get there? If you don't know where you are going in life, how will you know when (or if) you have arrived? In the end, the direction your life takes you will depend on the goals you set, the choices you make, the experiences you have along the way and how you respond to those experiences, and the amount of faith you have, both in yourself, but even more importantly, in God. All of these things are intangibles; your goals, your choices, your experiences, and your faith, mixed together, will produce a life experience that is totally unique to you. No one else can live your life or experience what you experience. That is why you can't afford to trust your life to luck. You have to decide how you're going to tackle life.

The way I see it, you can look at life in one of two ways. You can choose your path and accept the destiny, or you can choose your destiny and accept the path. What's the difference? In the first case, you take life as it comes, making decisions at random with no clear pattern or plan and hope that you end up in a good place in the end. In the second case, you first decide where you want to end up and then choose the life path that will take you there. If you want to arrive at a particular destination, you can't afford to leave the journey to chance; you have to base your life decisions on where you want to go.

You can choose your path and accept the destiny, or you can choose your destiny and accept the path.

My family was on the road a lot as we traveled from one place to another conducting ministry tours. When you're traveling, you have many different options in planning how to arrive at your destination. You can choose to stick to the freeway as much as possible. It's quick (most of the time), easy, and usually the most direct route to where you are going. If you prefer, you can choose to follow secondary roads: federal and state highways, county roads, and such. The trip will take longer because you will go through more cities and towns with their traffic lights, narrower streets, and more congested traffic. The upside to secondary routes, however, is that often they are more scenic, and because you are taking your time, you are able to enjoy the journey more.

In life, the freeway could be compared to the "fast lane," the easy road that carries no demands, no commitments, no responsibility, no accountability...and no future. It's over almost before you know it, and when you look back you have trouble remembering where you have been. There is no time to reflect, no time to think, no time to enjoy the journey itself.

Traveling the secondary road through life is more challenging, but richer because of it. In pursuing your goal, you will face many roadblocks; this way is highly demanding and requires a major amount of commitment, responsibility, accountability...and faith. As with every goal in life, your goal is personal to you, and every step you take, every decision you make, is an experience that will either take you closer to or further away from the successful future you hope for.

The key to a successful life and maintaining kingdom principles always starts with a solid foundation, a clear vision or focus, and again, the determination to run the race. Your life choices will determine your foundation. You can set your eyes on the goal and decisively plan your journey to its fruition or, like many, you can simply take life as it comes. You and you alone will choose the direction you want to travel and the foundation will conform itself to your decision. It is really kind of simple. Think about it. If you are building a building, it must be built on a solid foundation. As a matter of fact, if you have ever visited a construction site, you will notice that a large amount of the time, research, energy, and finances are put into creating a very certain and firm foundation that will surely uphold the structure that is about to be built. If the foundation is weak or flawed, it will only be a matter of time before the structure will begin to crack, crumble, and eventually collapse. Therefore, what good would it do to pour a lot of time, money, and energy into erecting a beautiful and elaborate superstructure on top of a flawed foundation that will give way and cause the entire building to collapse in a short period of time? It's the same way with life. You really have no choice; you are going to build your life upon some kind of foundation. The one decision you have to make is how solid your foundation will be, so you'd better be careful to lay a foundation that is solid and secure enough to hold you up.

However, the foundation for life is different than the foundation for a building. A building is fixed and immovable, but life is moving and ever-changing; therefore, every decision you make will either strengthen or weaken the foundation you have laid for your life. Faith is the only secure foundation for life, and you don't build a foundation of faith with your fleshly hands.

If you want a successful life with a bright future, you have to build your life on a solid foundation, and that foundation is Jesus Christ. With Christ as your foundation, you will have the strength, stability, and confidence to carry you through every situation, wherever life takes you.

Faith is the only secure foundation for life.

There are certain attributes that lead to a successful, happy, and prosperous life—attributes such as faith, hope, love, joy, and relationships. These words are very complex in that they are experiential words. We can give testimonials that include these attributes, but they cannot be truly explained; they can only be experienced on an individual level. The foundation upon which you build is a reflection of your own personal experiences and decisions.

Jesus never begged or pleaded for followers; He simply issued the call, laid out the requirements clearly, and let each person count the cost and make up his or her own mind. Here is an example:

> *As Jesus started on his way, a man ran up to him and fell on his knees before him. "Good teacher," he asked, "what must I do to inherit eternal life?" "Why do you call me good?" Jesus answered. "No one is good—except God alone. You know the commandments: 'Do not murder, do not commit adultery, do not steal, do not give false testimony, do not defraud, honor your father and mother.'" "Teacher," he declared, "all these I have kept since I was a boy." Jesus looked at him and loved him. "One thing you lack," he said. "Go, sell everything you have and give to the poor, and you will have treasure in heaven. Then come, follow me." At this the man's face fell. He went away sad, because he had great wealth* (Mark 10:17-22).

This young man knew the destiny he wanted—eternal life—but when he counted the cost, it was more than he was willing to pay. Instead of choosing the destiny of life and accepting the path of self-denial and obedience to Christ that went with it, he chose the path of self-indulgence and accepted the destiny of destruction that was its end. No wonder his face fell and he went away sad!

When I was five years old, I chose heaven as my destiny and accepted the path that God laid out before me. Of course, at that young of an age I did not fully understand all the implications of following Jesus, but I knew I loved Him and wanted to trust Him with my life. As I grew older and increased in my understanding, I tried always to be faithful to the Lord and walk the path He had given me to walk. True to His Word, He was faithful in bringing me into my eternal destiny. I am living it to the full now, more alive than ever before, so I can tell you with absolute certainty that all of God's promises are true. In the end, nothing in the material world counts for anything; Jesus Christ is all that matters. It doesn't work to build your life around temporal things because they never last. Even good things like family, hobbies, jobs, relationships, health, etc. are temporary in this world, and if you build your life around them you will be building on a weak foundation. Remember what I said about the sands of time running through our fingers? In the end there is really nothing to hold onto. Your hand is empty and the sand falls to the ground. It is extremely temporary and moves very fast. Our hobbies, jobs, relationships, and social status are all like the sand—here today and gone tomorrow. There is so much more to life than what we try to build and establish with our own two hands. But walking and experiencing the life of faith is what builds eternal value. The bottom line is that when your time comes and you

Walking and experiencing the life of faith is what builds eternal value.

stand before the Lord, the only thing that will really matter will be your relationship with Him. You may be surprised to find that He will not at all be concerned with the size of your home, your social status, your powerful job, and all the good things you have done in life. His only concern will be the depth of relationship that you experienced in Him during your brief time on earth.

Through all the various experiences of my life—through all the ups and downs, highs and lows, good and bad, joy and sorrow—Jesus was the rock, the central core of my life, who brought me security in uncertain times and filled me with peace that defied human understanding. There were many times when I was in the hospital for various reasons, and especially while awaiting my second heart transplant, that different members of the hospital staff and others expressed surprise and even amazement at how calm and at peace I was considering the monumental health challenges I was facing. I can't take any credit because that peace did not come from me but from the Lord. His peace filled my heart and took away my fear. I was calm and at peace because I knew the destiny I had chosen. I knew I was on my way to heaven and it did not really matter what happened to me on earth. Someone once said that the seed of fear is at the root of faith. This is going back to what I mentioned earlier. Because I was confronted with an opportunity where fear was lurking to overwhelm me, this was also an opportunity to grow in faith. I decided not to give in to that seed of fear and, by doing that, my faith was greatly strengthened during this time.

For me, faith in Christ was more than just believing some stories or a set of facts about a particular Jewish rabbi who lived 2,000 years ago. My faith was centered not on mental knowledge alone but also and most importantly on a personal love relationship with Jesus Christ. From the age of five, when I first acknowledged Jesus Christ as my personal Savior and Lord, He was the most important person in my life; more important even than my mom and dad. I know it won't bother them for me to say that because they would agree with me. Jesus Christ is the most important person in their lives also, even more important than me. And that's the way it ought to be. The word "Lord" means master and owner. If Jesus Christ is Lord, that means He is entitled to our fullest love and devotion, with no rivals.

After I gave my life to Jesus, I was hungry to know Him better. As I grew older physically, I also grew spiritually, reading my Bible every day, praying every day, both alone and with my family, and all the time gaining more and more knowledge of Jesus and what He expected of me. That personal relationship is the key. How can you trust in someone you hardly know? How can you walk by faith with someone you are barely on speaking terms with? I believe this is one of the main reasons why so many people struggle when faced with difficult times. They barely know Him because they hardly ever spend time with Him. They are not grounded in their faith or in their knowledge of the Lord and have never learned to trust Him in every part of life—big, little, or in between. When trouble comes, they try (and fail) to handle it on their own because they have never learned to stop trusting in their own resources or their own strength and place their trust completely in Him. Because they don't cultivate their relationship with Him during the good times, they are completely unprepared to face the bad times when they come.

A personal relationship with Jesus is the key.

Speaking of bad times, I know some of you are probably wondering right now how a good God could allow so much suffering in the world, particularly in the lives of people who love Him. I can hear you now: "But, Austin, how can you love and trust a God who would allow you to go through so much pain and discomfort, a

God who would let so many bad things happen to you?" My question to you is this, "Did God really want this to happen to me and does God really make bad things happen to people?" My answer is no. The truth is, we were all born into a sick and sinful world. Bad things happen—car accidents, house fires, the death of a child, cancer, and many other devastating tragedies. Whatever the case may be, these are things that I believe unfortunately are just a part of life. Let me share one of many stories that really gripped my heart when I first heard it. It was late one evening. A husband, wife, and children were fast asleep. The mother woke in a panic at the smell of smoke. Upon opening her bedroom door, she realized that fire had already spread throughout most of her house. In a panic, she escaped through her bedroom window and from outside the house began screaming for help. "Save my children!" she cried. "Save my children!" Shortly thereafter, when the fire crews responded, one child was rescued from an upper level bedroom. The mother still pleaded for the lives of her other two children, to no avail, as the firefighters fervently worked to extinguish the fire. The horrific news that two children perished was a blow that most simply could not understand. The question was asked, "Why would God allow something like this?" And at the funeral, statements were made such as, "God must have needed two more little angels." Although this story is very tragic and it broke many hearts, the truth is that God did not do this. It was an accident. A lit candle had gone out of control. Accidents happen every day, as well as other unexplainable tragedies such as school shootings, bully-induced suicides, murders, car accidents, and fatal illnesses—all of which I attribute to living in a sick and sinful world. The only thing that can carry the surviving family members through such difficult times is faith and a personal relationship with their heavenly Father. There are those who may spend the rest of their lives being bitter and hating God and there are those who, through their brokenness and tears, will hold firmly to the hem of His garment, trusting that He will see them through. Believe me, after you get here you will see how the difficulties in life grow dim!

Remember that after sin entered into the world, we were all born to die. Although sometimes we struggle when faced with catastrophic and untimely death, it doesn't change the fact that we were born to die. Our only hope in this world is realizing and accepting that Jesus is the Son of God and that He came to earth and died for us so that we could have hope in a world where there is no hope and the promise of eternal life with Him. Whatever situations you face in life, if you have your hand safely tucked in His, you will always find the strength you need to continue running your race. When you set a goal and keep your eyes steadfast on that goal, He will carry you through every difficult situation. Although it seems like a fairy tale in today's day and age, I can assure you that if you will center your life around God, build your life on the solid foundation of Jesus Christ, place your trust completely in Him as the Savior who died on the cross for your sins and as the Lord who is worthy of all of your allegiance, and surrender control of your life to Him, then He will give you life in all its fullness, life in its vitality, life that has no end. That is the life of a winner!

CHAPTER 10

I'M A WINNER
EITHER WAY

Throughout the pages of this book, I have shared many of the keys that I feel unlock the doors to a winner's life. And in my next book we will continue to discover winning keys, for I believe it is possible for everyone and anyone who accepts the challenge to be a winner regardless of life's situations. "A winner all the time and all the time a winner." Doesn't that sound good?!

I believe it is possible to find the silver lining in every cloud. This is more than just a statement. It is an attitude. And just like I said earlier, "God is good all the time and all the time God is good."

This has always been one of my favorite things to say. But in my heart, I believe that even on earth we can be joyful all the time and all the time we can be joyful. You may not find yourself feeling happy (since happy is an emotion), but you can still have joy even when you are full of sorrow because joy is an experience of your spirit and is not dependent on your circumstances. Finding thankfulness in every situation is the most important key to becoming a true winner.

> *Finding thankfulness in every situation is the most important key to becoming a true winner.*

In today's society, Christianity has been made out to be extremely complicated. And living a winner's life, to many, seems impossible. But the truth is, it is really not all that hard. As a matter of fact, most of the work has already been done for you. The price has already been paid for all who will commit themselves to the reality of living out their Christian walk, realizing their true purpose and potential, keeping their eyes on the goal, and running the winner's race.

We have shared together many topics such as being desperate for Daddy, the importance of a father/son relationship, and, more importantly, having a relationship with your heavenly Father. Just as a child is desperate for a daddy's love, strength, and approval, so the heart of a winner is desperate for a "daddy relationship" with his or her heavenly Father.

We have learned that God has no boundaries to His love and no restrictions to how He can help you. When you put your heart in His hands, you can trust Him through every life circumstance. Through the good, the bad, and the ugly, holding firmly to His hand, you will emerge a winner.

We also learned the importance of embracing our boundaries, of accepting our limitations and being joyful and thankful for who we are, the way we are. We have learned that regardless of physical, emotional, and mental boundaries, if we maintain that childlike wonder, hold firmly to His hand, and accept that He loves us just the way we are, regardless of any outward manifestation of weakness, God still has a perfect plan and purpose for our life.

In God's design, we each have what I call a "personal talent" DNA. Everyone has something special that he or she can do that no one else can do exactly the way he or she can. No matter how desperate the situation, maintaining a thankful attitude and trusting Him is the key that puts you right in the middle of the winner's circle.

We talked a lot about the transition to heaven. Perhaps we talked too much about this topic for some because, for many, talking about heaven is a scary thing. But we also learned that, once again, with your hand tucked safely in His, death has no sting. Although many spend their lives with the fear of death, we have learned that death is not really the end, but the open door to the beginning of our eternal destiny.

Whether we like it or not, we were all destined to die. Death is inevitable. We all have a choice to make. When that time comes, young or old, will we enter into eternity in the grip of the Father's hands?

We have learned a lot about faith, especially that faith is an experience. Faith is practically impossible to explain. We can talk about faith, but faith is really all about personal experience. Faith is ours to experience and it is impossible to experience someone else's faith. God's grace and mercy are sufficient and operate within each of us on an individual basis, according to our needs. That is why, even for me, some things are very hard to explain. I can simply share them with you, hoping that it will ignite your heart with a passion to experience the same faith relationship that I have been talking about. When we put our life in His hands and walk in faith, He is our protector and provider, and He loves us completely. We will find ourselves living in the center of His grace and mercy. That's what I call "the winner's circle."

> *In the center of His grace and mercy is what I call "the winner's circle."*

All of these topics have been designed and written to help us understand that we can truly live a winning life on earth. Whether in life or in death, we can be a winner either way.

I have really enjoyed sharing with you and I hope the feeling is mutual. My goal is simple: to help people around the world understand that "God is good all the time and all the time God is good." And that no matter what you face in life; in His hands, you are a winner.

I know that heaven is a very hard thing for many people to understand and I know that when you think about death many of you can't help but be fearful or upset. But I want to close by sharing just a little bit more about heaven. After all, it is my new home.

Heaven was a frequent and popular topic of discussion in my family. We talked about death and the process of dying and life after death. If somebody who did not know us or our situation ever happened to listen in on one of those family discussions, I guess he or she might think it was creepy. After all, what kind of family spends time talking about death? Here's the answer: the kind of family for whom death is more of an ever-present possibility than with most other families.

Because of Alisha's and my challenging and intense health issues, we were all aware that either she or I could go at any time. In fact, we understood that death could take any of us suddenly and without warning. So we talked about it. Mom and Dad wanted to make sure that we were prepared for all of life's eventualities, but most of all for eternity. In today's society we have taken heaven, and especially hell, out of the equation. The idea of hell, to many, seems almost absurd and extremely unrealistic. As a matter of fact, when was the last time you went to a funeral and heard the words, "heaven" or "hell"? These are words that most of us seldom hear at a funeral. It is more common to hear, "They are finally at peace," or, "They have gone to a far better place."

Many have lost sight, not just of the reality of heaven and hell, but also of the reality of God. We try to live a faith-based life in a world that demands explanation and information. Faith, like I shared previously, goes beyond explanation. It is a matter of the heart.

The concept of heaven and hell, God the Creator, and Jesus the Son of God are concepts that become impossible to believe without faith. Therefore, many people, even Christians, have drifted far away from the true purpose of the cross. Faith believes in something that you cannot always grasp intellectually and in many cases is extremely hard to explain. Remember, faith is an experience, and to experience true faith, you must first experience a relationship with God.

Heaven and eternity are even more difficult concepts for many to truly understand.

Instead of really believing in the existence of eternal life, they live in a hope that there is eternal life. Let me say this: If there were no heaven and hell, then there would be no God. So, to believe in God is to believe that there is a heaven and there is a hell. And where we spend eternity will be based on the choices that we have made in our life. Everybody dies. Not everybody goes to the same place. The choices we make during our life on earth determine our final destination and where we will spend eternity.

Everybody dies. Not everybody goes to the same place. The choices we make during our life on earth determine our final destination.

Although it is true that we talked about death more than most families, it was always in the greater context of talking about life. For a Christian, someone who has given his or her life to Christ in faith, death is not the end. Neither is it something to be feared. Death is merely the doorway from a lower dimension of life to a higher dimension of life. If you are a Christian, there is no reason for you to fear death because, live or die, you are a winner either way. There is a song we liked to sing as a family in our ministry concerts that contains these words: "I'm a winner either way, if I go or if I stay, for I still have my Jesus each passing day. I'll have my healing here below or life forever if I go. Oh, praise the Lord, I'm a winner either way." [2] In other words, if you are a Christian, you cannot lose. All your options are good. No matter what you face in your earthly life, your eternal future in heaven is assured. It is a win-win situation.

Take it from me, the closer you are to death, the more precious heaven becomes. The closer you get to heaven, the less appeal the things of the world have on your heart. For a Christian, life on earth is good, but heaven is better. Facing death and eternity, for many, can be like a tug-of-war. If life is filled with love, joy, and prosperity, it may be very hard to let go and make the journey to the other side. You can't help but think about what you are leaving behind, especially your family and friends.

I felt that tug-of-war in my own heart more than once. On the one hand, I loved my family and wanted to stay with them, but on the other hand there were times

---

2. "I'm a Winner Either Way" by Laura Colston Lewis/
Trina Curtis/Chestnut Mound Music.

when I was so sick and the struggle was so hard that it seemed to me that it would be such a relief just to let go of my life so I could be with Jesus. Well, now I am with Jesus and I can tell you that this definitely is the better option! But the timing of my departure from earthly life was not mine to determine. When God knew it was time, He called me, and I could not ignore His call.

We used to talk about how we could not know which one of us would be the first to go. It could be Dad, Mom, me, or one of my sisters. Because of the desperate medical situation we were facing, the reality of death was ever-present and age did not matter.

I never obsessed over death, but I probably spent more time thinking about it than most young people my age, simply because I knew it could be close at hand at any time. I also had no fear of death because I knew where I was going and that heaven was a far better place to be than earth. At night I would often listen to a recording of the Book of Revelation as I went to sleep. John's beautiful prophetic picture of heaven and the life to come really whetted my appetite to go there. But I also learned the art of living for today. Too many waste so much time revisiting the yesterdays and worrying about the tomorrows. I have learned to live each day as if it was a lifetime and that today is all that really matters.

When my time finally came on that October day in 2010, I did not greet death with a heart full of fear. I simply walked through the doors of my eternal home. The transformation was awesome. Instantly, in the twinkling of an eye, my body was filled with new life and the pain and suffering was gone. I can run. Boy, can I run! Sometimes I think I could fly. I am truly alive. And yes, you heard me right. In death I am alive and I am whole. I have run my race and won.

So, in life or death, you can be a winner either way if you are in Christ. That means death is defeated, your destiny sure, your victory certain, and heaven secure!

If you have given your heart to Christ, you are a winner either way because you have nothing to fear in either life or death. Either way, you belong to the Lord and He will carry you through.

For a Christian, death is not the end, but only a doorway to a higher dimension of life that is rich, full, vibrant, and joyous beyond your wildest imagination! All of history has been leading up to the day when creation will be renewed and the sons and daughters of God revealed in glorious immortality, fulfilling the eternal destiny He planned for us since before the foundation of the world!

And if you allow Him to be Lord of your life, you too can say, *"I'm a winner either way!"*

You can contact the Mullett family at:

P.O. Box 275   Penrose, NC 28766

themullettfamily@gmail.com

www.themullettfamily.com

www.imawinnereitherway.com

Also available are four CDs
recorded by the Mullett Family:

* "Knowing What I Know About Heaven"
in honor of Austin Trent Mullett

* "Blessing the Lord"

"For His Glory"

"From Test to Testimony"

Visit their website for more
information or how to order.

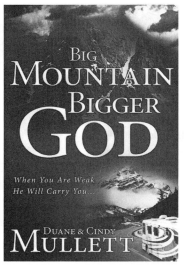